Praise for **YOUR SHOPPING SUPERPOWER**

T0357383

"Whether for your health, or for guidebook shows you how to unle world you want each time you sho Diane as my mentor for decades and her experience in ethical shopping is unsurpassed. In her own words, 'Now in a world that seems to have lost heart, you can shop with yours.'"

—**Julia Ormond,** actor and human rights activist

"It's difficult to shop our way out of the climate crisis, but we can organize, connect, and make a difference. In this practical guide, Diane Osgood helps us see that we are not alone, and that collective action is not just possible, it's essential."

—**Seth Godin,** founding editor, *The Carbon Almanac*

"Balance your buying with your beliefs. In this wise book, learn steps to minimize toxicity and harm to our Earth by harmonizing your values and your choices."

—**Elena Brower,** author of *Practice You* and *Hold Nothing*

"We all have the power to change the world through the products we buy. Here's a guidebook that shows you how."

—**Paul Rice,** founder and CEO of Fair Trade USA

"Every time we buy, we vote. This timely guidebook empowers us as shoppers to demand good jobs of dignity, clean non-toxic products, and a restored environment"

—**Ayesha Barenblat,** founder of Remake (www.remake.world)

"This is a must-read for anyone wanting to leverage their purchase power to build a better world. Diane created the required field manual for responsible purchasing, converting passion into practice. She made it simple for us."

—**Justin Dillon,** founder of FRDM and Slavery Footprint

"A timely masterpiece! A powerful, fact-based work backed by thirty years of experience. Essential reading for our times—insightful, practical, and much needed."

—**Diana Verde Nieto,** business leader and sustainability expert, author of *Reimagining Luxury,* and co-founder of Edify Collective

"The sleeping giants for a better world are consumers. The language of business is profits and the big influence on governments is business. It all derives from people consuming goods. It is rare for a book to offer the why, what, and how, but Diane Osgood has done it in this book! She has done it brilliantly. It delves into discovering values-based shopping guides that will engender happiness and empower people to discover their responsibility for a better world—and it is clear and readable."

—**Fuzz and Carolyn Kitto,** co-directors of Be Slavery Free and The Chocolate Scorecard

YOUR SHOPPING SUPERPOWER

Follow your values and better your world one purchase at a time

DIANE OSGOOD, PhD

Health Communications, Inc.
Boca Raton, Florida

www.hcibooks.com

Library of Congress Cataloging-in-Publication Data
is available through the Library of Congress

ISBN-13: 978-07573-2526-7 (Paperback)
ISBN-10: 07573-2526-2 (Paperback)
ISBN-13: 978-07573-2527-4 (ePub)
ISBN-10: 07573-2527-0 (ePub)

Publisher: Health Communications, Inc.
          301 Crawford Boulevard, Suite 200
          Boca Raton, FL 33432-3762

Cover, interior design, and formatting by Larissa Hise Henoch.

In memory of my parents,
Joe and Carla Osgood

For future leaders
Adelaide, Erin, Gloria, Miriam,
Ondine, and Victor

CONTENTS

Chapter 1
UNLOCK YOUR SUPERPOWER... 1

Chapter 2
SHOP WITH YOUR VALUES TO BOOST YOUR HAPPINESS.................... 11

Chapter 3
DETECT GREENWASHING, SEEK TRUSTWORTHY CERTIFICATIONS, AND AVOID PERFECTIONISM.. 23

Chapter 4
PEOPLE: BUY FROM BRANDS THAT TREAT PEOPLE FAIRLY................. 41

Chapter 5
PLANET: BUY ENVIRONMENTALLY RESPONSIBLE PRODUCTS............ 79

Chapter 6
COMMUNITY: BUY LOCAL AND FROM BUSINESSES WITH DIVERSE OWNERSHIP... 117

Chapter 7
HEALTH: SHOP TO AVOID POTENTIAL HEALTH HAZARDS.................. 147

Chapter 8
KEEP COSTS DOWN 195

Chapter 9
SHOP NEW WAYS.. 207

Chapter 10
CONCLUSION: SHOP AS A FORCE FOR GOOD 217

**APPENDIX: FIND THE INFORMATION YOU'RE LOOKING FOR ON
COMPANY WEBSITES** 225

NOTES 239

PERMISSIONS 261

INDEX... 263

ACKNOWLEDGMENTS 276

ABOUT THE AUTHOR 279

Chapter 1

UNLOCK YOUR SUPERPOWER

If you care about the planet, the people who make your things, your local community, or your health, this book is for you. It will guide you to unleash your shopping superpower so that your choices help protect the planet, create better jobs for more people, foster community, and protect your family's health.

I discovered my shopping superpower while studying wild orangutans in Kalimantan, Indonesia. Watching the tropical forest cut down before my eyes, I understood in a flash that if no one bought products made from tropical wood, there would be no market for this timber, and deforestation would stop. My realization was simplistic, but it fueled my desire to pursue this work, earn a PhD at the London School of Economics, and become an authority on sustainable and ethical products.

For more than thirty years, I've helped companies innovate to manufacture and sell sustainable products that are better for the planet. I advise CEOs from many name-brand companies, presidents and prime ministers, fashion icons, and celebrities. I'm a sustainability nerd with the passion to empower you, the consumer, to find and use your shopping superpower as a force for good.

Enough about me. What about you? As you pick up this book, chances are you don't want your food exacerbating climate change, your clothes stitched by slaves, or your family exposed to harmful chemicals. Yet many shopping choices lead to these unintended outcomes.

Through my work, I've learned and compiled tricks, tips, and strategies to help you align the contents of your shopping cart with what matters most to you: a kinder, healthier, and more sustainable world.

I wrote this book to help you unleash your hidden superpowers, make the world a better place, and increase your happiness and well-being. This book shows you how to shop intentionally. You'll learn how to choose products that are kinder to the planet and made by companies that treat their people fairly. You'll see how easy it is to protect your family's health by selecting products that are free from potentially harmful chemicals. Discover ways to support your community through local, women-owned, and minority-owned businesses. Learn which changes in shopping maximize impacts, what certifications and rankings to trust, how to recognize greenwashing, and other tips and tools to make it easy to find the products and brands that align with your values. You'll keep your family safe and feel good about your purchases.

Shopping with your values makes you happier. It sounds cliché, but when you realize that you can align your spending with the kind of world you want, it feels good. You're not a victim of big corporations that pollute the oceans and destroy forests. You get to choose, for example, if you want to support women who own businesses or companies that don't put harmful chemicals in your face wash.

Shopping with intention also benefits those beyond you and your family. Your choices help create lasting positive impact. About 60 percent of the U.S. economy is driven by consumer spending.[1] When you purchase something, you send a positive signal to the market: "I'll have more of that, please." Companies hear your signal and continue to make more of the same product, under the same conditions. Your spending—when combined with others' spending—shapes what companies produce and how they treat workers, the environment, and local communities. This in turn impacts which sectors of the economy grow and which shrink.

Most of the environmental damage and labor abuse caused by companies making our stuff can be stopped. For example, Levi's discovered new ways to use substantially less water in manufacturing jeans and even shared its know-how with competitors, yet most companies still haven't committed to significantly improve how they make products. Companies will not change their behavior until they are forced to do so—that is, when shoppers like you make the problem too painful to ignore.

If you stop buying products made in ways that appall you, you reduce demand for those products. When enough people stop buying these types of products, the maker will either discontinue them or find ways to improve how they're made. With AI and big data, brands track and monitor shifts in shopping behavior closely.

It's surprising how few people it takes to change a company and transform an entire industry. The first time I saw dolphins caught in tuna fishing nets, I felt nauseated. Millions of dolphins were being caught in gill nets and drowned. Feeling compelled to fight this horrible fishing practice, I volunteered with a nonprofit organization called Robin des Bois (French for Robin Hood). Burning with outrage, I wanted to board boats to force the fishermen to stop. But Robin des Bois had another plan—to enlist consumer pressure. Fueled by strong coffee and flaky croissants in a tiny eco-chic office in Paris, I helped organize letter-writing campaigns to ask shoppers to stop buying dolphin-killing tuna. Since fewer than one out of one hundred consumers took part in this campaign, I felt discouraged and frustrated that I'd wasted my time. Yet eighteen months later, we received stunning news: The world's three largest tuna-canning companies made an unprecedented decision to stop buying tuna caught with nets that also catch dolphins. The companies said they changed their practice because of consumer pressure. Goliath met David.

You can make a difference without organized campaigns—because signals from shoppers like you encourage companies to expand their positive efforts. For example, in 2019, the J. Crew Group launched its first Fair Trade Certified collection for the Madewell brands. Why? Their customers wanted it. Fair Trade Certification matters because it means that jeans are made in factories that pay fair wages, ensure safe working conditions, and offer equal opportunities. Fair Trade Certified jeans cost more for Madewell to make because the labor is more expensive than in sweatshops. However, Madewell didn't pass along the higher costs to shoppers.

It's normal to feel a bit overwhelmed when you try to make shopping choices that protect you and the environment, and the workers who make what you buy. It's a complex task because most of the things you buy have complicated origins. For example, think of your favorite sweater—it left footprints around the world long before you laid eyes on it. Most likely, the wool came from one country and was sent to another country for dyeing and knitting into fabric. The sweater was stitched by people in a factory in a third country, then shipped and sold to you by a retailer. At any stage, workers may have been abused or paid unfair wages. Dyeing fabric uses vast amounts of clean water and often toxic chemicals. These chemicals can impact the health of the people working in the factories, and factory runoff often escapes into local waterways.

Friends often ask me which are the most sustainable and ethical jeans, laundry detergent, knitting yarn—you name it. Their questions led me to write this book. It covers the issues that most shoppers care about:

- People: Buy brands that treat people fairly.
- Planet: Buy environmentally responsible products.
- Community: Buy local and from businesses with diverse ownership.
- Health: Shop to avoid potential health hazards.
- Costs: Keep costs down.

My goal for this book is to inspire and equip you to consistently buy products that support what you value, starting with the issues that matter most to you. By choosing one topic, it's easier to start and stay focused. My bet? It will also likely make you happier and more content with what you purchase. You'll find evidence of this in the next chapter.

Of course, buying organic fruit, fair trade coffee, and certified sustainable paper will not immediately solve climate change or end slave labor. These are complex, entrenched problems. Yet each shopping decision you make sends companies a signal. With each choice, you can help us all move toward making a better, safer, and more just world.

An important note: This book isn't about buying less. The virtues of buying less are many. It's the first "R" of the 5-R Rule: Refuse, Reduce, Reuse, Recycle, and Repair. Guidance on how to buy less is covered in many wonderful books about living simply and with less.[2] This guidebook helps you when you choose to buy something new.

YOUR SUPERPOWER PRINCIPLES

If your shopping superpower feels overwhelming at first, apply these three principles to shop with purpose:

1. No rights, no wrongs.

    There isn't one set of "right" priorities or "right" choices that applies to everyone. Your neighbors, friends, and cousins may be motivated by different issues than you are. Focus on what matters to you.

2. Start close to your heart.

    Select an issue that you care deeply about. Make one shopping change a week to address this issue. For example, if you place a high value on fairness or equality, you may decide to focus on how workers are treated. The first change you make may be to buy Fair Trade Certified chocolate. Next week you can add another fair labor product to your list— say, coffee or that new pair of jeans you've been eyeing.

3. Progress, not perfection.

    Perfection is a long way off. At some future moment, all products may be ethically produced and environmentally restorative, ushering in fair treatment of all workers, and supporting local economies. Until then, focus on making steady progress, one purchase at a time. Focusing on progress also protects you from feeling despair.

HOW TO USE THIS BOOK

In Chapter 2, you'll learn why unleashing your shopping superpower can make you happier. Greenwashing brands attempt to deceive you by marketing false claims of sustainability and ethical business. In Chapter 3, you'll learn how to detect greenwashing and avoid being duped by brands.

Chapters 4 to 7 cover four key topics: people, planet, community, and health. The first part of each chapter tells the story of what you buy, which will help you determine what matters most to you. You'll start with one area of focus and one simple change each week. Over time, you'll apply these tools and tips to more shopping choices. Then it starts to roll downhill like a snowball. These four chapters can be read in any order. For example, if you are excited about a specific topic—such as supporting women-owned businesses—start with Chapter 6.

The second part of each chapter gives strategies, tools, and tips to easily shop for products that avoid harm and promote solutions. The tips include how to

- Make one impactful change a week.
- Seek trustworthy certifications.
- Use ratings systems and apps.
- Avoid the worst offenders.
- Tell the brands you care.

Each of these four chapters ends with a summary table for easy decision-making for the most impactful changes you can make for frequent and occasional purchases.

People—Buy Brands That Treat People Fairly

People make most of your stuff. Sure, robots play a part in some production lines, but it's mostly humans who stitch your clothes, harvest the crops you eat, and screw together the parts in your electronics. People pick and pack items in warehouses, load trucks, and make deliveries. Many of the people who helped make the products you buy aren't paid fair wages, and they work in dangerous conditions. There isn't one simple measure or way of summing up a company's track record for how it treats employees and contractors. That's why I break it down for you in Chapter 4. In this chapter, you'll find tips and tools to make shopping decisions based on how brands treat workers.

Planet—Buy Environmentally Responsible Products

All products come from natural resources. Even a chunk of plastic starts out as a fossil. The fossil is transformed into fuel that is turned into plastic. Water, land, minerals, forests, and biodiversity are needed to make just about everything. Want to buy products that are less damaging to nature or buy from companies that actively help restore the environment? In Chapter 5, I describe the different types of environmental impact, including climate change, deforestation, biodiversity loss, excess water use, and waste. Emerging regenerative approaches to agriculture and materials pave the way forward with promises to greatly reduce the environmental impact of some products. The tips and tools in this chapter can help you make better shopping choices to reduce your impact on these facets of the environment.

Community—Buy Local and from Businesses with Diverse Ownership

Shopping locally creates a virtuous cycle for your community. Locally owned businesses tend to create good, local jobs. Shopping locally means more of your money stays in your community. On average, forty-eight cents out of every dollar spent at a local, independent business is recirculated locally, compared to less than fourteen cents from purchases at chain stores. Keeping three times more money circulating locally means more jobs and more tax dollars that stay in your community.

Buying from women- and minority-owned businesses is a powerful way to address underlying economic inequalities based on gender, race, and systemic poverty. You have power to support these types of businesses, so why not use it? In Chapter 6, you'll find easy ways to identify locally-owned, women-owned, and minority-owned shops and businesses. You'll also find suggestions for supporting other people you may not have considered—such as refugees, people with disabilities, and the previously incarcerated.

Health—Shop to Avoid Potential Health Hazards

Chemicals found in food, cosmetics and personal care, household cleaning products, and clothing may impact your and your family's health. You may not know that you're inadvertently eating harmful toxins or applying known carcinogens to your face. According to the nonprofit organization Environmental Working Group (EWG), at least a dozen "dirty food chemicals" are found in products on U.S. grocery store shelves. This list is longer for cosmetics, clothing, and household cleaning materials. Luckily, as you'll see in Chapter 7, it's relatively easy to make healthier choices.

Cost is perceived as a big barrier for many people who want to purchase more sustainable and ethical products. Chapter 8 dives into the cost of shopping with your values and provides actionable tips to keep costs down. Chapter 9 looks at new shopping models, including renting, borrowing, and buying products from peers. Warning: These methods may lower your costs and increase your enjoyment.

The final chapter of the book summarizes top priority switches for frequent and occasional purchases. The Appendix provides detailed information about what to look for on a company's website.

Unlocking your shopping superpower is a rewarding journey, but at times it can be hard. I still struggle sometimes. One day I may want that shiny bracelet even though I have no idea about the brand's labor or environmental standards. Other times, especially when traveling, fair labor and environmentally responsible options aren't available. For example, I can't always find Fair Trade Certified or rainforest-friendly coffee at an airport or hotel. Throughout this book, I share my own confessions of compromises and trade-offs I've made when faced with hard choices.

Let's dive in.

Chapter 2

SHOP WITH YOUR VALUES TO BOOST YOUR HAPPINESS

Through a store window, a pair of red leather boots with three-inch heels winked at me. In my early forties, I wanted to feel sexy. Magnetized, I went into the shop. My heart pounded lightly, and I felt a rush as I tried them on—perfect fit. I winced when I read the label "Made in Bangladesh," but I didn't let that get in my way. The sales lady quickly rang up the boots, and by the time I got to my car, the rush had slunk away. I felt a thunk in my heart as false narratives sprang to mind. "It's the price of beauty." "One pair doesn't matter." "I'll wear them for years."

I had my boots, but the joy was gone. I couldn't erase the pictures in my mind of boys in torn shorts and flip-flops with red dye running down their arms. Nor the sight of girls and young women stitching shoes in cramped factories so dangerous that when one collapsed, it killed more than 1,100 factory workers.[3]

I wore these boots for a few months but gave them to a charity shop because wearing them made me feel guilty—not sexy.

A few years later, a black sweater caught my eye on Instagram. It was luxurious, naturally black alpaca made with fair labor practices and crafted to last. The sweater was stunning, as was the price—almost double what I'd expected.

So I took a few days to think about it. On the brand's website, I discovered it's a B-Corp—a certified sustainable company—owned and run by two women committed to creating intentional, long-lasting clothing from organic fibers. The brand supports artisans and upcycles its fabric scraps.

That's when it hit me. Here's a brand that makes beautiful clothing and shares my values. I swallowed hard. It was time to put my money where my mouth is. I ordered the black sweater.

Years later, I'm still wearing it and feeling proud of my choice to buy it. Each time I wear this artisan's creation, I feel like I am receiving a warm hug in return. Its production contributes to a better world where more people earn fair pay, chemical dyes are avoided, and natural resources are conserved. All this makes me happy. Since the sweater embodies what I value, I feel connected to the brand and want its founders to continue to succeed.

Wearing the sweater also makes me feel sophisticated, nearly glamorous, even when I'm in old jeans and having a bad-hair day. The deep-black alpaca glistens in the sunlight—and the shimmer isn't from a chemical treatment.

This chapter explains why shopping with your values boosts your happiness. Learn about the following:

- how dopamine impacts your shopping experience
- how your shopping choices can boost your happiness
- why you like what you choose
- how to avoid happiness busters while shopping

SUGAR HIGH, SHOPPING HIGH

Shopping highs are real. Dopamine is the happy chemical, and shopping activates the areas of your brain that release it into your system. Dopamine is a neurotransmitter that makes you feel good, and it's linked to searching for pleasure and rewards.

Online shopping creates rushes of dopamine because you have to wait for the purchase to arrive at your doorstep. Waiting builds anticipation, which increases the dopamine trigger. This is why many shoppers report getting more excited over buying online than in-store.[4]

Any unpredictability in a reward increases the amount of dopamine released. It is the thrill of the hunt. Log onto your favorite online store or walk into your favorite boutique—you'll feel it. The simple act of starting to shop tells your body to produce more dopamine. Your brain searches for pleasure and rewards, and the chemicals rush to make shopping feel good.

The link between unpredictability and dopamine makes sale prices alluring. Sales—especially massive events such as Black Friday—provide the perfect set-up for a big dopamine rush. Why? Your dopamine runs wild because of a sale's added thrill and suspense, making the anticipation much sweeter. The rush of delight makes it hard to resist buying—whether you need to buy or not.

The fear of missing out on a deal also affects the brain. While shopping, your mind might switch into competitive mode. You must be the first to have it—the new color, the new style, the latest updated piece of tech. Another mind trick is scarcity—the story that if you don't buy it now, you won't be able to get it later. Of course, marketing amplifies these mind states.

All this adds up to a cocktail in your brain: one-part anticipatory dopamine, a splash of unpredictability, followed by a twist of competitive mode or scarcity impulse. Shake this up with the pressure of a time-limited sale, and you have a potent dopamine cocktail.

Dopamine reinforces rewarding actions. That's why, once you buy one item—for example, what you went to the shop or online to buy—you're often tempted to buy more, even if you don't need the items. It works the same with cookies.

But just like a sugar rush, the shopping high is often followed by a crash, leading to buyer's remorse. Buying with your values helps you alleviate the roller coaster of ups and downs to avoid such a crash. Neurochemical research suggests the experiences that create upbeat vibes can blunt dopamine-triggered impulses. Shopping with your values can be such an experience, bringing you a prolonged sense of happiness and releasing a positive neurochemical counter to dopamine. You gain greater control over your impulses to buy more stuff. The long-lasting positive emotions I experienced from buying the black sweater helped me resist the dopamine rushes triggered by discounts or targeted Instagram marketing.

HAPPINESS AND MONEY

Money can't buy you happiness. But making purchases that align with your values can. Deeper and longer lasting than a hit of dopamine, true happiness comes along when you:

- act in accordance with what you value

- are generous
- connect with community
- are grateful

When your behaviors match your beliefs, you are in alignment and more connected with yourself, so you experience less internal friction. The less internal friction, the more ease and flow. You are who you say you are. You do as you say you do—including the narrative you tell yourself about yourself. Decisions are more comfortable and quicker because you know where you stand. There is less to fret over.

Acts of kindness and generosity can increase happiness, optimism, and satisfaction. There is evidence that helping others promotes physiological changes in your brain linked to happiness.

Choosing items made by fairly paid workers is an act of generosity. Fair pay provides families a livelihood and a way beyond survival hood. As you'll read in Chapter 4, many brands, large and small, support fair trade wages. For example, Michelin, the company that makes tires and car parts, announced in 2024 that all employees will receive remuneration at least equivalent to a living wage. Michelin's paying a "decent wage" impacts 132,000 workers in twenty-six countries. Unilever and L'Oreal recently made similar pledges, as have many other companies.

Connecting with communities fosters happiness. It evokes a sense of belonging along with personal and collective identity. It boosts self-esteem and your power to make your dreams happen. There are several ways to connect to a community. Frequenting local shops and taking time to chat is one simple way. Getting to know who made your things or grew your food lifts your heart. During the pandemic, my local farmers' market was my lifeline. Brief conversations with the vendors made me feel sane and connected to my community. These are essential conditions for happiness to flourish.

Many years ago, my husband, George, and I went to the Heard Indian Fair and Market in Phoenix. After touring the show, we chose two coffee mugs. We chatted with the artisan, Mel Cornshucker, a Cherokee potter from Tulsa. A few months later, I wanted to surprise George with another piece by Mel, but I'd lost his business card and couldn't find his website. How could I find him? Sleuthing paid off, and I tracked down a gallery representing him in Chicagoland. The owner confirmed that Mel doesn't sell online because he hates shipping his pieces. Luckily, the gallery had a bowl about the size I wanted, and I bought it. Over the years, the gallery owner informed us when Mel was coming to town for a pottery show, and we always tried to connect with him. Our visits grew to include shared meals and gentle laughs. He accepted our request to make us a set of dinner plates with dragonflies—one of his signature designs—and we agreed to pick them up in Tulsa. When we sit down for dinner, the dragonflies remind us of our friend Mel.

Gratefulness

Gratefulness drives happiness, not the other way around. Gratitude helps you realize that what you have is what you want. When you feel grateful, there is no room for magical thinking about what could be. You are content with what you have. Gratitude combined with happiness helps keep you in a state of "enoughness." Like being sated after a fabulous, flavorful meal, you are satisfied. Being sated, you can counterbalance dopamine-driven impulses to buy more. Gratitude is also a powerful antidote for feeling any sense of lack or want. It saves you from the thousand paper cuts of scarcity that plague many people.

You Like What You Choose

You like what you choose. No, that is not a typo—this really happens. Your brain says, *I chose this, so I must like it. I didn't choose this other item, so it must not be as good.* Your mind justifies your choices after a purchase.

New research confirms that random choices lead to preferences. It follows that intentions lead to habits because you tend to choose the same thing over and over again. Given that you justify your choices after the fact, what you like is formed by habit.[5]

This is good news. You don't need to change what you like. Intentionally change what you buy instead, and your preferences will follow.

Suppose you consciously choose to swap a conventional product for a climate-friendly good. In that case, your brain will trigger, and you will like it. Initially, it might require overriding opinions about the product's characteristics, such as price or style. But old opinions will fade as you form new shopping habits.

The Stories We Tell and Other Happiness Busters

You may often tell yourself stories about what you buy to assuage guilt. These stories are seldom anything more than a justification or excuse to purchase something you know deep down doesn't align with your values or the type of world you want.

"Me buying one plastic bottle of water isn't going to make a difference to climate change or ocean plastics."

"Not buying one cheap T-shirt isn't going to end child labor or abusive factory conditions."

"Buying a toy online isn't going to put the local toy shop out of business."

Climate change, plastic waste, underpaid factory workers, and the demise of local shops are complex issues that take persistence to resolve. One single purchase will not save the day, and indeed, the impact of a single purchase may barely be felt. But what you do and tell yourself about your actions matters for two reasons.

First, you can stop being part of the problem and signal positive behaviors to others. Refusing to buy cheap T-shirts made in conditions that are most likely dangerous for workers isn't going to resolve the wage crisis many factory workers face. But buying one will contribute to the problem, and others will take their cues from you. If you are okay with wearing fast-fashion clothes, it is also okay for others. Carrying your own water bottle rather than buying a plastic one isn't going to stop climate change, but it is going to help. You will not contribute to more plastics made from fossil fuels and discarded in landfills or waterways. Furthermore, others will see you and your action, which helps to set off a positive chain of social validation.

Second, you're not being honest with yourself when you tell yourself misleading stories. You're contradicting the part of you that makes ethical decisions. Each contradiction slowly chips away at your self-esteem and confidence. It's not worth it! Furthermore, guilt feeds on these false narratives. You tell yourself a story to feel okay about buying something, but then you feel even worse for lying to yourself about it. This path does not lead to happiness.

False narratives can rob you of your chance to bring your deeply held values to life. And that is a real loss.

Out of Sight, Out of Mind

It's easy to diminish the impact of our choices because we live at a physical and cultural distance from the people who make our clothes, toys, and food. Even if you've seen images of sweatshops, it's hard to comprehend what the working conditions are truly like. It's an empathy stretcher.

The best antidote is to learn more. Check out websites such as Remake, Environmental Working Group, The Carbon Almanac, and organizations mentioned in this book.

To counterbalance confidence-crushing stories, try this:

1. **Talk back to the story.**

   No one else will notice if I buy conventional rather than fair trade coffee beans, chocolate, or bananas. You and your self-esteem will notice.

   Buying from a local boutique costs more, and I can't afford it. Have you checked the prices? Cost might be a real barrier but double-check the actual price difference. Often buying local comes with a similar price tag to equivalent items online. You also can touch the item—feel the quality or check the size. By buying local, you'll save time and shipping costs on returns. More on cost saving in Chapter 8.

   This sweater, jacket, shorts, or hat is so cheap, I just have to have it. It's cheap for a reason. Do you really want to support unfair wages to buy something at that price point? Do you want to support a company that thrives by mistreating the environment or workers?

It's better that factory workers have any job, even if it's poorly paid and dangerous. No, that's worker exploitation. Don't you prefer to buy from brands that pay fair wages?

2. **Don't feel badly if you go ahead with a purchase.**

    Admit to yourself and accept that, in this moment, you're making a compromise. *I am buying this because* . . . , then forgive yourself quickly. Next time, you might make a different choice. But for now, accept the compromise and move on, leaving guilt behind. You'll find examples throughout this book of how I make compromises. It's not possible to make the best choice all the time. Remember to focus on progress, not perfection.

3. **Focus on adding one change a week.**

    Keep change manageable and know that over time you'll change what you buy and what you like.

DEEPER REWARDS

When you start shopping consistently with your values, more profound rewards await you. First, your internal sense of your role in the world changes from bystander to empowered citizen in the economy. Reject what's bad for you, your family, the planet, and the people who make it. You're not a consumer who accepts whatever companies thrust onto the market. Choose products that support your wellness, create better jobs, and restore the environment.

You know what you expect from a company, and what is a deal killer. Shopping becomes an exercise in active and conscious choice. This frees you. You are no longer susceptible to the wiles of marketing and dopamine chemical rushes. You discover that your choices have far-reaching consequences, because what you buy influences what companies make and retailers stock.

You also get to support people who do what they love. Your purchases can support entrepreneurs following their dreams. For example, a weaver in upstate New York gets to continue creating stunning handwoven fabric from cotton, linen, and silk because enough people value her work. The jacket made from her fabric feels like wearing a hug. Farmers get to continue farming the land their families have held for generations because of their loyal customers. A woman can grow her hair-care company from side hustle to full-time job and provide excellent employment for other women in her community.

Consider this: A baker follows her passion to make bread. Your purchase enables her to continue baking. When she sells a loaf to you, she is saying, "Thank you for enabling me to do what I love." With your purchase, you are saying, "You're welcome," to the baker. Happiness blossoms when you and the baker both gain from the trade in ways far more meaningful than just the money. It's a rich exchange.

Happiness comes from feeling connected to what you know is essential and what you hold dear. Right now, it may feel that's a bit much to consider when buying the mundane necessities of life such as carrots or diapers. Still, as shopping with your values becomes integrated into your life, it becomes a part of your daily flow. If you have a gratitude practice, consider pausing to be thankful for all the people and nature involved in bringing to you what's on your table, in your closet, and on your feet. I promise it will bring a smile to your face.

Chapter 3

DETECT GREENWASHING, SEEK TRUSTWORTHY CERTIFICATIONS, AND AVOID PERFECTIONISM

When Kourtney Kardashian announced her sustainable collection with Boohoo, a fast-fashion empire, I almost spat out my morning coffee.

This news was greenwashing at its worst: a trendy celebrity launching a "sustainable" fashion line with zero substance behind the claims. Arriving at Boohoo's offices by private jet demonstrated Kardashian's cluelessness about sustainability. The partner she chose, Boohoo, has ranked among the worst in the fashion industry for environmental and social performance.

Boohoo churns out fast fashion in record time, creating mountains of textile waste while doing little to reduce hazardous chemicals and greenhouse gas emissions.[6] It has a track record of treating factory workers poorly. In 2020, Boohoo's UK-based factories paid less than five dollars an hour. It also sourced from sweatshops in Pakistan that paid workers as little as forty cents an hour.[7]

Boohoo's campaign sought to woo customers and distract critics with glamorous photo shoots of Kardashian. It didn't work. Outraged, activists and shoppers loudly pressured Boohoo to improve. Kardashian started listening to sustainability experts, and the company claims it has made amends with bold goals and improved reporting. Yet, in 2024, the company continues to rank at the bottom of the fashion industry,[8] and a group of investors brought a lawsuit against Boohoo because they suffered losses brought on by allegations about labor rights violations in Boohoo's supply chain.[9]

This chapter sets the foundations for making better choices. You'll detect which products and brands are taking real action and which are bluffing. Learn

- how to detect greenwashing
- which certifications to trust—and which to ignore
- why trade-offs are necessary, and why perfectionism is the enemy of progress

GREENWASHING AND BLUEWASHING

Deceptive marketing is all around us, and it can distort the environmental and ethical attributes of a product or brand. It works because shoppers rely on visual cues, emotions, and social trends rather than checking the facts. These deceptions are called *greenwashing* when applied to environmental concerns and *bluewashing* when applied to social issues. Regardless of the color, such marketing disrespects you, the shopper.

Brands often use words and images to suggest you are buying something good for the environment. Greenwashing involves disingenuous marketing, including changing an existing product's packaging to look greener, stating vague claims, and adding images of plants or nature scenes.

Greenwashing includes ambiguous or disingenuous product information. For example, a 2022 investigation found that fashion giant H&M showed customers misleading environmental scorecards for some of its clothing. The company took down the scorecards and apologized.[10]

Brands use bluewashing because they want to sound more ethical or socially responsible than they are. It's sometimes called *social washing*. It happens when a company obscures an underlying social issue to protect its reputation. Brands mislead on social issues such as labor standards, racial justice, human rights, product safety, data privacy, and diversity, equity, and inclusion. For example, a brand may donate to social causes—such as a children's hospital—without the social cause bothering to ensure that there's no child labor used in the manufacture of the brand's products.

Bluewashing is on the rise, particularly on the issue of pay equity. For example, many companies release social media statements about female empowerment on March 8, International Women's Day. However, most companies that post platitudes conceal their own significant gender pay gap.[11]

Easy Ways to Detect Greenwashing and Bluewashing

Deceptive marketing persists, but you don't have to fall for it. Here are four ways to avoid being duped.

Be Suspicious of Feel-Good Imagery, Vague Terms, and Color Coding

The easiest way to detect greenwashing and bluewashing is to check for misleading imagery and vague terms. Watch out for green leaves, nature scenes, and buzzwords such as "natural," "farm fresh," "eco-friendly," "fair," "responsible," "ethical," or "LGBTQ-friendly." For example, many bottled-water brands show nature scenes on their labels. This is laughably ironic, considering that plastic water bottles are designed to be single-use, and plastic waste creates massive environmental problems.

Be wary of blanket statements. Rather than looking for a product that says nontoxic, biodegradable, or clean, seek out products that say exactly what they are; look for specific statements such as 98 percent organic ingredients, fair trade standards, no palm oil, or 100 percent postconsumer recycled materials.

Color can be a tip-off. Some brands use green and earthy tones to promote eco-friendly products.[12] Some brands use blue labels and color palettes that suggest responsibility, trustworthiness, and purity—the reason most bottled water packaging is blue.[13]

Tip: Watch out for common greenwashing and bluewashing buzzwords, the most common of which are in Table 2.1.

Table 2.1. Common Greenwashing and Bluewashing Buzzwords

Treatment of People	Planet and Nature	Health Characteristics
Conscious	Eco-friendly	Clean
Ethical	Farm-fresh	Natural
Fair	Green	Nontoxic
Responsible	Natural	Safe

Look for Relevance

Be suspicious when a company makes a big deal about one aspect of green on an otherwise totally ungreen product. For example, it's greenwashing when a nonrecyclable plastic toy comes in cardboard with "recyclable packaging" buzzwords printed all over it.

Similarly, McDonald's made a lot of noise about being "environmentally responsible" when it introduced paper straws in Europe and Latin America. Did the straws make a dent in the waste created by the fast-food giant? Of course not—and worse, these straws turned out to be nonrecyclable.[14]

Be wary of audacious goals that miss the point. Coke set a goal that 50 percent of its bottles would be made from recycled material by 2030.[15] Sounds impressive. However, a 50 percent decrease in an ever-increasing number of single-use plastics bottles is not a viable solution for the planet. Coca-Cola is the world's largest plastics polluter and fails to address the heart of the matter—its dependence on single-use plastic bottles.

Tip: Remember the big picture. What are the brand's significant environmental and social issues, and does the claim address them fully? Or is the brand's action like swatting a single flea on an infested elephant?

Mind the Gap: Incomplete Information

Some brands obscure the truth by leaving out key details of how their products are made or what they are doing to protect people and the planet. You can't detect this while comparing products in a grocery store or an online retail site. Catching this form of greenwashing requires checking the brand's website. The Appendix gives you the details of what to look for. Here's a summary:

Check out what companies say about sustainability, responsibility, purpose, or any similar phrase. Go to the home page, and if there is no mention of caring about people or the planet, look under the "About" tab or at the bottom of the home page for a "Sustain-ability" link. When a brand is opaque in its reporting and communi-cations, it's difficult to verify its claims.

Table 2.2. Checklist of What to Look for on a Company Website

Trustworthy	Questionable
Clear, relevant time-bound goals, e.g., to reduce greenhouse gas emissions by 60 percent by 2030 from a 2020 baseline	Vague, open-ended goals, e.g., "carbon neutral" or insignificant goals, e.g., reducing plastic straw use but keeping nonrecyclable single-use cups
Third-party certification for meeting labor or environmental standards	No third-party validation of efforts or standards
Transparent listing of product ingredients and explanation of how they are selected	Doesn't list all ingredients. Ingredient standards are not shared.
Commitment to highest standards across all countries and market segments	Applies the lowest possible legal standards in each country.

Tip: Look for European products to lead the way in clear environmental and social communications. European countries are cracking down on terms such as "carbon neutral" and "net zero carbon emissions." Companies using these terms in Europe need to meet rigorous standards or become liable for greenwashing.

Lack of transparency is the trickiest form of deception to identify as a shopper. Common practices include cherry-picking the rosiest facts, focusing on less relevant data, and obscuring the complete truth with blather. In the most unethical cases, companies even lie or fabricate data.

How to spot it? The easiest way is to pay attention to what is said about the company by trustworthy news media. For example, journalists cracked the case of Volkswagen deliberately falsifying its emissions data.

In addition, be skeptical of bold claims. Check the brand's website for evidence of an audit or third-party verification. Claims of achieving 75 percent carbon reduction in three years make my eyebrows arch in disbelief. When you see such claims, dig for evidence.

The Sad Case of Volkswagen (VW)

Once famous for VW Bugs, VW is now infamous for falsifying emissions data on about a million diesel cars. VW's green marketing focused on fuel efficiency, yet its claims were based on fake data. Caught in 2015, the company was fined $2.8 billion by a U.S. federal judge for cheating emissions tests and deceptive advertising. However, the greenwashing scandal is estimated to have cost the company more than $32 billion in lost reputation and sales.[16]

Stardust in Your Eyes—Watch Out for Celebrity Endorsements

Celebrity endorsements often work. They increase shoppers' positive response to "green" and "ethical" products.[17] But does the celebrity touting a brand have the chops to make a claim? Or is it celebrity-washing?

To avoid falling for celebrity-washing, ask: Does the celebrity have a reputation as an advocate for human rights or the environment? Have they taken a public stand on environmental or human rights causes? Have you ever heard them discussing these or similar issues when they're not endorsing a product?

While it's tempting to dismiss all virtue signaling of stars, award-winning actors such as Naomi Watts and Emma Watson have earned trust. Watts developed her street cred to advocate for clean beauty by submerging herself into the nontoxic beauty world for many years. Watson's deep understanding of and advocacy for sustainable fashion led the French fashion conglomerate Kering (which owns Gucci, Yves Saint Laurent, Stella McCartney, and other brands) to choose her as a board member. She became chair of Kering's sustainability committee, championing circularity and new eco-minded designers.

In general, steer clear of products that have celebrity endorsements unless you find evidence of a celebrity's actual expertise on the topic. Look for interviews and articles that indicate the star is meaningfully engaged in the topic, be it child labor, water, renewable energy, or ocean plastics.

Trust Your Gut

If your gut tells you something is fishy and doesn't add up in an advertisement or social media posting—trust your gut instinct. If the messaging rings false, it probably is. For example, panda bears or sprouting plants are mascots of greenwashing because they tug at heartstrings. If you see something on a package or advertisement that touches your heart because it feels warm, fuzzy, green, or socially responsible, pause and look closer for more details. Does the label or advertisement explain what is meant? Does it have a trust badge or certification mark? If you see no details, either look for another product or delve deeper to verify your hunch.

TRUSTWORTHY CERTIFICATIONS

One of the quickest ways of determining whether a brand's claims are legitimate is to check for certification marks. Certification marks are trust badges that tell you what's good about a product. They appear as small logos. You'll find one or more placed on the front, side, or bottom of a package. Each indicates the product has met the standard of a particular certification.

Certifications vary, depending on whether they cover environment, fair labor, diverse business ownership, or nontoxic products. Watch out if you see an eco-label you've never heard of, and do some digging to ensure it's not bogus. Brands sometimes invent logos or marks that resemble authentic certifications for environmental or social standards. That's why it's essential to look for trustworthy marks.

160 Million Reasons to Buy Certified Products

"As my two vibrant daughters returned to school after summer break, I reminded them how darn lucky they are even to be able to go to school. There are at least 160 million children around the world toiling instead of learning—half of them in hazardous conditions from the carpet looms of India to the cobalt mines of the Democratic Republic of the Congo. So as consumers, we have at least 160 million reasons to 'vote with our dollars' to buy a GoodWeave-certified handmade rug and help ensure that at-risk kids can learn and play," explained Jon Jacoby, CEO of GoodWeave International.[18]

GoodWeave works to stop child labor in global supply chains. It assures no child, forced, or bonded labor is used in the making of a certified product, and the certification also means your purchase supports programs that educate children and improve working conditions for adults in producer communities.

Which Are Trustworthy?

Not all certifications are equal. Some are gold standard and credible, and others are green- or bluewashing. The differentiating factor is who issues the standard and verifies that the product or brand meets the standards. Certifications are issued by corporations, independent organizations, or a collaboration of the two. As explained below, a standard made up by a group of companies is less trustworthy than one created and verified by an expert independent organization. You'll find three types of certification standards: certification marks issued by expert independent organizations, company-led collaborations with third-party verification, and company-designed marks.

Certification Marks Issued by Expert Independent Organizations

These certifications are the most trustworthy because an independent organization monitors and audits the brand or product, using specific environmental or ethical standards. A product or brand that meets these standards can carry the certification mark.

Certification bodies are usually specialized nonprofits with deep knowledge of the issues. They don't bow to pressure. Sometimes a government agency issues standards—for example, USDA Organic and ENERGY STAR. Often called "third-party run and verified" standards, they are the gold standard for certification.

Some certifications cover an entire brand while others cover specific products. The Fair Trade USA, Leaping Bunny, GoodWeave, and Rainforest Alliance marks are awarded to specific products, such as jeans, eyeliner, and coffee. The Butterfly Mark is a third-party run and verified certification for ethical and environmentally sound luxury brands, such as Dior Couture, Kiehl's, and Tag Heuer. The certification process checks brands, rather than individual products, against a range of environmental and ethical standards.

Company-Led Collaborations with Third-Party Verification

Some companies develop their own environmental or labor standards rather than adopt existing ones. To ensure rigor, these companies collaborate with nonprofits to help define the standards and verify compliance.

This is a middle-of-the-road approach. It's trustworthy. However, the company still controls the design of the program. It can design less-demanding standards than those set by third parties, or it can allow loopholes. At the same time, the standards can't be set too low or allow large loopholes because the partnering nonprofit would walk away.

For example, Starbucks Coffee Company created its own C.A.F.E. standards for its coffee, which includes standards for farmer equity. It developed the program with a global verification body, SCS Global Services, and a well-established environmental nonprofit, Conservation International. In addition, coffee farmer compliance is verified by independent organizations. C.A.F.E. standards are loosely in line with other environmental certifications but don't require as much assurance of fair pay to farmers as Fair Trade Certified and Fair for Life do.[19]

Company-Designed Marks

Some companies design their own certification scheme, create a mark, and stick it on their products. It's hard to gauge how robust and trustworthy these marks are. Are they real or are they just marketing? Without good partners to lend trust and provide some credibility, you must rely on the company's word.

For example, Cocoa Life is a program run by the international conglomerate Mondelēz International. The program aims to improve cocoa productivity, empower communities, and conserve and restore forests.[20] Mondelēz's chocolate brands made with cocoa sourced from these communities display the Cocoa Life mark.[21] However, it's hard to gauge the program's effectiveness because the company does not indicate if any outside experts or organizations have validated their program. Is it bluewashing? Without more transparency, it's hard to tell.

The diagram below sorts out different types of certifications, showing different options, depending on whether the certifier is a company or an independent organization.

Types of Certifications

CERTIFIER	VERIFIER	SUBJECT	CERTIFICATION	PRODUCT
Third-party organization >	Disclosed third-party >	Product >	Fair Trade Certified >	>80% of Patagonia's clothes
		Brand >	Butterfly Mark >	Kiehl's
			Woman Owned Business >	Vosges Chocolate
Company >	Disclosed third-party >	Product >	Starbucks C.A.F.E. Standards >	>95% of Starbucks' coffee
	Company or Undisclosed third-party >	Product >	Mondelēz Cocoa Life >	Toblerone

Avoid company-designed marks because it's hard to determine whether they're real or bogus marketing ploys. A disclosed third-party verifier is essential for any certification mark to have much credibility. In addition to these certifications, industry-wide collaborative programs work toward systemwide change. These programs address the roots of the problem—whether it's sweatshop working conditions, water pollution, or the use of toxic materials. The programs usually don't provide a certification mark for individual products or brands because they focus on improving the overall system, not just a specific product. For example, the International Labour Organization's (ILO) Better Factories program seeks to improve working conditions in factories making apparel and footwear for global brands. It brings together brands, factory owners, and sometimes unions to upgrade pay, workers' health and safety, and gender equality. Similarly, the Leather Working Group brings companies and suppliers together to address the environmental impacts of leather production. In Chapters 4 to 7, you'll learn more about these types of issues and programs.

Where to Find Certified Products

You can find certified products—from jeans to cans of tuna—pretty much anywhere you shop. You can look up specific certifications—say, Rainforest Alliance's Green Frog certification—and find the list of brands that meet their standards. You can also check your local retailers. Grocery, fashion, sport, and furniture retailers sell certified products and brands along with uncertified ones. For example, you'll probably find Rainforest Alliance certified Dole brand bananas sold next to regular, uncertified Dole bananas.

You'll find certified products at retailers such as Target, Walmart, and Costco. For example, all of Walmart's own-label coffee is third-party certified, and Target sells fair trade GoodWeave-certified rugs next to uncertified rugs. Your purchase sends a clear signal to the retailer that you'd like the retailer to expand certified options.

Never hesitate to ask a retailer for certified products. For example, if you want a sofa or other household furnishing made with fair labor standards, ask the retailer which items are certified by Fair Trade USA or Nest. For energy-efficient appliances, ask to see products with ENERGY STAR ratings. It's a double win. By asking, you'll find certified products and signal to the retailer that you care enough to ask.

Chapters 4 to 7 discuss which certifications to trust for people, planet, community, and health—and how to spot them quickly.

NOTHING IS PERFECT—DON'T LET IMPERFECTION STOP YOU

The world is complicated and messy. No brand is perfect. No certification process is flawless. No human is 100 percent consistent. All products leave footprints, some positive and many negative. Look for better, not for perfect.

The process by which our stuff is made is complex. Much of what we buy is made overseas, or in the United States with imported components. What happens overseas is hard to monitor. Bad things happen overseas—and at home. In January 2024, two underage teens were found doing dangerous work in a meatpacking facility near Detroit.[22] This is the tip of the iceberg.

One enslaved person is one too many. One more poisoned river is unacceptable. Thinking of the impact of one more plastic water bottle in the ocean makes me want to scream—or cry. In an ideal world, these issues would have been long resolved. Children would be protected, workers would be fairly paid, and all products would help regenerate the planet. All products would be made and sold in a way that creates better jobs for more people, a healthier planet, and better health for all. But we are many years away from that scenario.

The quandary of perfection is deeply personal for me, as I've worked for more than a decade on ending slavery in supply chains. I've met entrapped workers, talked to them in the baking sun, and felt their desperation. How could I justify supporting any product or brand that isn't 100 percent certain to be free from this evil crime? Sadly, I no longer believe that any product can claim to be 100 percent slave-free because supply chains are complex, and corruption remains persistent.

For the most part, abuse is allowed to continue because top executives are too disconnected from what happens on the ground. Greed is a powerful force, especially when combined with voluntary blindness.

"Don't confuse perfection with excellence," warns Julia Ormond, Emmy Award–winning actor and antislavery activist.[23] "Crimes of slavery and labor abuse are highly emotional, and it feels abhorrent to accept them at any level," she says. "But if we expect perfection, we will get disheartened and be derailed. If we expect excellence, improvements can be both incremental and urgent."

Labor abuse, environmental damage, systemic discrimination, and corruption are hard to solve because they evolve and require a systems approach—which is why it's so important that companies work to address root causes.

Regardless of certifications and progress, necessary trade-offs arise daily, with no perfect choices. Take, for example, leather and wool. They are wonderful materials, especially in chilly winters.

Tanneries create toxic waste, and cows and other livestock account for a whopping 12 percent of all greenhouse gases.[24] What are the alternatives? Most vegan leather is made from virgin plastic—which is made from climate-warming fossil fuels. It's also not nearly as durable as animal-skin leather. Similarly, acrylic fleece jumpers made from recycled plastic bottles shed microplastics into our rivers and oceans every time they are washed. The result? When you want to buy something, there will be trade-offs.

All the tips and tools in this book have flaws. Activists and perfectionists are quick to point out the weak spots and failures of any certification. At the time of writing, investigators in Brazil recently found evidence of abusive and unsafe labor practices at coffee farms allegedly covered by C.A.F.E. standards.[25] With enough boots on the ground, could Starbucks have found the coffee farms' unethical and illegal labor practices earlier? Perhaps. The Brazilian farms blend their beans at a cooperative, which then sells to Starbucks, Nestlé, and others, making traceability difficult. Starbucks took a stand. Love or hate Starbucks, they changed the coffee business for good by creating standards. When I can't find Fair Trade Certified, Fair for Life, or Rainforest Alliance coffee, I'll buy at Starbucks rather than at a massive conglomerate that isn't doing the hard work in its supply chains.

Many brands work hard to improve production, reduce or eliminate pollution, and lift up workers. The executives of these companies are invested in what happens on the ground throughout complex supply chains. In the following chapters, you'll find out why this matters, plus tips and tools to find brands and products that have made big efforts to improve their impact. It's imperfect, but solid progress.

"Perfection is the enemy of almost everything that's important," Emma Watson said about sustainable fashion. You will choose again and again how to vote with your wallet. The only way to go is forward. Forward moves us from what we have now to an imperfectly better world.

Consider this when you find yourself stuck or annoyed at the lack of perfect alternatives: Progress isn't a handful of people shopping with their values perfectly. It is millions of people doing it imperfectly, together making a bigger difference in the world.

Chapter 4

PEOPLE: BUY FROM BRANDS THAT TREAT PEOPLE FAIRLY

Watching each step, careful not to step on embers, I walked through scorched sugarcane fields to reach the men cutting the cane. My nostrils stung from the acrid, sweet smell in the air. Even under the brim of my hat, my face reddened from the sun. In each field I'd find about twenty boys and men, from teens to men well past retirement age. Few had a hat or shoes, and I saw no signs of the protective gear the company had provided. Most wore torn clothes and sandals made from old tires. No one had a water bottle, sunglasses, or food. All of them were muscular, yet very, very thin. From morning's first light until dusk, these men cut cane with machetes, loaded it onto a wagon, and returned to cut more. They burned the cut fields behind them, adding to the heat of the day. The next day they got up and did it again. Due to systemic poverty and irregular immigration status, they have no path to permanent residency or citizenship. If the men and boys don't work, there is no pay, no food, no medicine. The cane cutters and their families are not slaves. Yet they are trapped in a system with few ways out for themselves, their families, or future generations.

Our goal was to conduct the first-ever field survey of these cane cutters. The sugarcane company we surveyed has since made significant improvements to working conditions. It's now certified by multiple globally recognized sustainability standards for sugar production. The company is also helping workers to regularize their status and gain permanent work permits. However, other sugarcane companies in the region—and in other countries—continue keeping workers under slavelike conditions. My heart still aches for those men and boys.

Many of the people who help make your products are not paid fair wages, and they work in dangerous conditions. It's unjust, and yet sadly common. Furthermore, women workers are often paid and treated even worse than men, and women are more vulnerable than men to harassment in the workplace.[26]

Most men's jeans sold in the United States are made in Mexican garment sweatshops, known as *maquilas*. Workers as young as fourteen cope with unsafe working conditions, intimidation, and violence, even sexual assault.[27]

Workers like Reina, who started working in a maquila when she was fourteen, want respect, safe working conditions, and fair pay. In an interview with the nonprofit organization Remake she asks, "What about the brands? I know they have codes of conduct. But they are not interested in the lives of the workers or conditions of production."

Abusive treatment of workers is inexcusable. More than twenty-five years ago, when I started working with companies on factory and farm working conditions, I was overwhelmed. Abusive labor practices were commonplace. Brands were just beginning to wake up to their responsibilities. Visionary leaders—from companies, labor movements, and nonprofits—stepped up and created new ways for brands to collaborate with factory and farm owners, improve working conditions, and ensure fair wages. Today all companies have the ability to protect human rights and ensure fair working conditions for the people who make their products if they want to do so. For example, companies don't have to buy from factories or suppliers with unfair or dangerous working conditions. Brands can buy from factories that have undergone training and are certified to a certain standard of care for their workers. When abusive or unsafe conditions are reported, brands can move production to facilities with better protection for workers. Alternatively, brands can stick with problematic factories and help them participate in programs to improve labor conditions.

Low wages and dangerous working conditions are not a matter of "better than nothing." Factories and the brands that buy from them are taking advantage of poor people who have no choice but to work for any wage, under any working conditions. And while many *workers* don't have a choice about working in abusive conditions, *you* can choose not to buy products that are made this way.

I start this chapter with the backstory of how certain products are made. You'll learn how to

- make informed shopping decisions to support the workers who make your things
- identify companies that strive to meet goals for a more diverse workforce, equal opportunity, and equitable pay

The tips in the second section help you find companies and products made by workers who are fairly treated and from companies that value a diverse workforce.

THE COMPLICATED BACKSTORY OF OUR BELONGINGS

Many companies and workers are involved in producing your things. Although the brand name might be Gucci, Levi's, or Trader Joe's, other companies are contracted to help produce and manufacture the products. They hire the people working at the factories, warehouses, and farms. A brand holds some responsibility for the working conditions of all the workers involved in making what they sell because they choose which agents, companies, and factories to work with.

The multitude of companies, factories, and suppliers involved in making a brand's products—such as a T-shirt or box of cereal—is called the brand's supply chain. Supply chains are often complex and work across many countries.

The diagram below shows a simplified journey for an item of clothing, from raw material to the final customer. Each step may occur in a different country. For example, denim is often washed and dyed in one country, then cut and stitched in another.

The Supply Chain for Garment Production

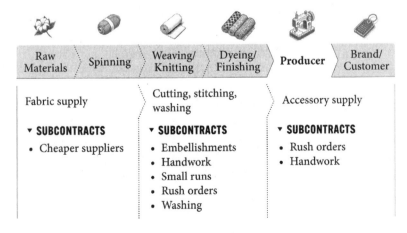

Supply chains include webs of subcontractors and subcontractors' subcontractors. Producers often hire subcontractors to get certain jobs done, usually washing, cutting, embellishments, handwork, and rush orders. If your T-shirt has an embroidered patch on it, the handwork was most likely done by a subcontractor. It may have been done by homeworkers. Another subcontractor may have been hired to stitch the embroidery patch onto the T-shirt, then return it to the original factory for folding, packaging, and shipping to the warehouse or store.

Who Put the Sequins on Your Shirt?

The demand for handcrafted items is booming. Increasingly, people want authentic handmade crafts for home furnishings, toys, and fashion accessories. More than 300 million home-based workers make pottery, baskets, home décor, embroidery, handwoven fabrics, quilts, and rugs for global markets. The work offers women flexible working hours. It also can provide appropriate opportunities for older children to work after school. Many home-based workers also do piece work, such as assembling component parts for toys, clothing, shoes, and basic household goods.

However, home-based workers are particularly vulnerable to exploitation. Who controls the hours and determines the pay? Do they have to work far into the night? Are children exploited and kept from school?

For handicrafts, brands can participate in certification programs such as Nest. Nest assures that home-based workers are paid fairly and work in safe environments, and that any children involved also go to school. And when you see certifications on the brand's products, you can be assured as well.

Unfortunately for component work such as light assembly jobs, no certification process currently exists to oversee these workers. It requires the brand to engage deeply with suppliers to understand when subcontractors employ home-based workers and to require that fair and safe work conditions are met.

Brands Call the Shots

Brands make choices through their purchasing practices that shape their products' journeys from the raw materials to the finishing trim and packaging. How purchasing departments interact with suppliers greatly impacts the labor conditions in factories and stress throughout the entire system. For example, last-minute change orders or a rush job can push suppliers to force overtime or hire subcontractors. Designs that require a lot of handwork in apparel, toys, or home furnishings can also lead to placing rush orders with in-home subcontractors, which increases the risk of exploiting workers to meet deadlines.

Brands often hire agents to buy fabric or component parts. Agents also contract with factories. These deals include an agreement on the brand's standards for quality, timelines, and shipping dates. The factory needs to provide assurance that it doesn't make knockoffs to sell on the black market. And, of course, the price is negotiated. During negotiations, the brand can insist that its standards and codes of conduct will be met for worker pay and working conditions. Ensuring that those standards are actually met is tricky—but at a minimum, it's a brand's responsibility to make contracts that stipulate fair wages. These agreements usually cover subcontractors, although the brand often has no line of sight into what work is subcontracted.

Some brands do a better job than others at mapping their entire supply chains and disclosing that information on their websites. This is becoming more necessary as brands respond to European regulations. Many have improvement goals for mapping and transparency. Collaborative initiatives such as Better Buying enable suppliers to rate brands, providing invaluable feedback for brands that seek to improve.

Supply Chain Workers: Wages, Safety, and Working Conditions

About 60 percent of apparel and other textiles are manufactured in developing countries.[28] In addition to wages, health, and safety, a long list of challenges faces workers in many factories: cramped and unsafe factory-owned dormitories, sexual harassment and violence, no time off, no medical care, and chronic malnutrition. Some employers hold onto their workers' documents, so the workers cannot leave. Recruiters for these jobs often demand fees, putting workers in debt and forcing them to stay on the job to pay back this debt—a form of forced labor.

Wages are central to the fair treatment of workers. A wage for full-time work should enable a person to meet their basic living expenses. Unfortunately, no global standard for a minimum or fair wage exists.[29] Some companies pay a "living wage,"[30] which is higher than the legal minimum wage because it's adjusted to the local cost of living.

Yet millions of workers around the world are paid wages too low to cover basic necessities and live with dignity. For instance, only

7 percent of the world's garment workers earn enough to cover food, rent, healthcare, and school fees for their children. Since the start of the COVID-19 pandemic, 75 percent of garment workers report that they have gone into debt to buy food.[31] Inadequate wages lead to malnutrition, no healthcare, unsafe housing, and high levels of debt and anxiety.

Safety is also a concern for many workers who are in constant danger of injury because of insufficient safety precautions and unsafe working conditions. Some workers toil through twelve-hour shifts and suffer the indignity of being chained to equipment or forbidden to take rest breaks. Many are exposed to toxic chemicals. Factories often lack basic safety equipment, such as fire extinguishers or emergency exits. Forced overtime can be dangerous, as well as cruel, because exhausted workers have more accidents than those who work shorter shifts.[32]

Moving work to low-wage countries is a strategy used by many companies to cut costs.[33] For example, if having T-shirts made in China becomes too expensive, the apparel company might look at factories in Cambodia or Ethiopia, where wages are lower. In Ethiopia, apparel factory workers earn a base salary of about $26 a month, which is well below the $110 monthly minimum wage estimated for a person to afford the basics in that nation.[34] In addition to low pay standards, some of these lower-wage countries also have higher risks of labor abuse.

Fast-fashion companies rely on low wages and quick production times because they create new clothes each week to entice constant sales. Bangladesh is the number-one producer of fast fashion. The collapse of the Rana Plaza factory building in 2013, which killed 1,132 garment workers, sparked global outrage over unsafe working conditions and low pay.[35] This outrage led to significant attempts to reform oversight and accountability in Bangladesh's garment industry, but the results are mixed.[36] Some brands support reforms in Bangladesh and neighboring Pakistan. The nonprofit organization Remake tracks the brands that support such reforms and which companies signed the International Accord for Health and Safety in the Textile and Garment Industry, a legally binding agreement between garment and textile brands and trade unions to facilitate factory safety in countries without strong safeguards.

Environmental Certification and Labor Practices

Some other environmental certifications, such as the Rainforest Alliance Green Frog certification, include a fair labor requirement. Others don't. For example, the USDA Organic certification does not cover working conditions and pay. However, if a farm or factory has gone through the effort of obtaining organic certification, it's a pretty good indicator that they also take care of their employees.

Some fair labor certifications include a component of environmental stewardship. For example, Fair Trade USA ensures that farms pay fair wages and work to improve soil and water quality, avoid harmful chemicals, manage waste, and reduce greenhouse gas emissions.

Do Modern Slaves Make Your Products?

Slavery means that a worker is not paid and cannot leave by threat of violence. Child labor is forced labor if it keeps children from school or exposes them to perilous risk. Slavery and child labor have been found in almost every country in the world, including the

United States. Today, about 28 million people are enslaved worldwide. As many as 160 million children toil every day, almost one out of every ten children in the world. Because of poverty, 79 million children do hazardous work.[37, 38] They may chip rocks to produce the mica in sparkly eyeshadow, pick the cotton to make sheets, or dig in dangerous mines to collect minerals for electronics.

Child Labor and Forced Labor Hot Spots

LATIN AMERICA

Sugarcane
Belize, Bolivia, Brazil, Dominican Republic, Mexico

Gold
Peru

Coffee
Colombia, Costa Rica, Dominican Republic, El Salvador, Guatemala, Mexico, Nicaragua, Panama

AFRICA

Diamonds

Gold

Minerals
Burkina Faso, Central African Republic, Democratic Republic of Congo, Sierra Leone

Cocoa
Cameroon, Ivory Coast, Nigeria, Guinea, Ghana, Sierra Leone

Coffee
Kenya, Sierra Leone, Uganda, Ivory Coast

Tilapia
Ghana

ASIA

Cotton
China, Azerbaijan, Kazakstan, Turkmenistan

Electronics
Fireworks
Toys
China

Textiles
(embellished)
China, India, Nepal, Thailand, Vietnam

Carpets
Pakistan

Shrimp
Thailand

Slavery is hidden. Unless a company is actively working to ensure fair labor standards, it may not know what is happening out of sight in the depths of its supply chains. Some companies are aware of the risks and still do nothing to check—remaining willfully ignorant.

In recent years, slavery and abusive child labor have been found in cotton picking in Xinjiang province of China. Slavery and abusive child labor have also been found in Central Africa in mining for metals that go into electronics, and in tuna fishing for popular brands of canned tuna. It's not only low-cost products that come with these problems. Advanced electronics manufacturing is also rife with violations of workers' rights. A large amount of the manufacturing is done in parts of China that have state-sanctioned forced labor.[39] In Tip #4 below, you'll find a summary table of products to avoid that have high risks of labor abuse.

Forced Labor in China

Chinese cotton and tomatoes from Xinjiang province are banned from import into the United States because of high incidences of forced labor. U.S. Customs and Border Protection found evidence of debt bondage, restriction of movement, isolation, intimidation and threats, the use of detainee or prison labor, and situations of forced labor in China's Xinjiang region. Most of the victims are reportedly Uyghurs, an ethnic minority in China, who have been forcibly exiled to Xinjiang. Xinjiang produces more than 20 percent of the world's cotton, much of which is exported to other Asian countries, where it is blended into fabrics. This is where applying the law gets tricky. In 2024, some of these blended fabrics were detected in garments sold in the United States,[40] underscoring the difficulty of tracing a product's supply chain all the way back to fiber and farm.

Not all child labor is far away, in a country on the other side of the world. A 2023 investigation by the *New York Times* interviewed 100 documented migrant children in twenty U.S. states working arduous and dangerous full-time jobs, often at night. The investigation estimated that more than 100,000 unaccompanied migrant children work full-time. The children are exhausted, often frightened, and behind in schoolwork. They cut chicken in meatpacking plants, package snack food in massive factories, and handle heavy loads in commercial laundry facilities. This is illegal child labor happening today in the United States. The number of undocumented children working dangerous jobs is not known.

There is, however, an important nuance: Not all child work is illegal child labor. For many families, the extra income from their teenager working a few hours a week helps the family out of poverty or to pay for college. A child working a few hours a day, in a safe environment that doesn't interfere with school or put the child in any danger, can be okay. You may have had an after-school or weekend job busing tables, picking crops, or babysitting.

But children who work must be able to continue school and do their schoolwork. Working full night shifts that leave a child exhausted and falling asleep in the classroom is not acceptable, in the United States or anywhere. Every child harvesting cocoa with machetes, butchering chickens in a meatpacking plant, or staying up all night making auto parts is a victim of child labor.

The Case of Child Labor in Bangladesh's Leather Industry

Bangladesh's leather and tanning industry tends to dodge public scrutiny. Tanneries spew toxic chemicals into surrounding waterways and expose workers—including children—to a wide array of hazards. This is a massive export industry, with $1 billion in annual revenues.[41]

Curing and trimming hides for leather is dangerous work. Hides are soaked in chrome salt baths, pressed by heavy conveyors and rollers, and then trimmed by hand. Bangladesh's tanneries are forbidden to employ children under eighteen, yet they do. Journalists have documented fourteen- and fifteen-year-old boys—in flip-flops, baggy clothing, and no gloves—lifting hides soaked in chrome salt onto their shoulders as they carry them from one stage of production to the next across a slippery floor. Child workers reportedly earn between $1 and $2.50 per day.[42] That buys some rice and either a few eggs or vegetables, but not both. With the cost of a small apartment averaging about $80 a month, families can't afford safe housing on these low wages, much less school fees or healthcare.[43]

That's why illness and accidents—sometimes fatal—are common among tannery workers.[44] Loose clothing gets caught in machinery, and toxic chemicals burn skin. Untreated tannery waste is full of toxic chemicals, and exposure to acid dyes can be fatal. When tannery waste poisoned the Buriganga River, the government moved the tanneries to new facilities, but the problems moved with them. Solid wastes from the tanneries now pollute the Dhaleshwari River. Child labor has not been resolved, and workers remain without basic protective gear.[45]

Where Your Designer Handbag Came From

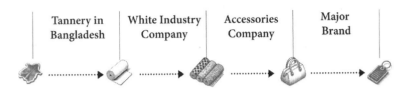

| Tannery in Bangladesh | White Industry Company | Accessories Company | Major Brand |

Major fashion brands, including Armani, Bass, Coach, Hush Puppies, Hugo Boss, Picard, and Timberland, source leather and leather goods from Bangladesh.[46] These fashion brands don't buy directly from the tanneries. Instead, the tanneries sell leather to a consolidator, and the consolidator sells the leather to a white-label factory that makes shoes, handbags, belts, and other accessories for many fashion brands. A white-label factory takes orders from fashion brands, produces the design and quantities requested, and then stamps or stitches the name of the brand onto each product.

In some instances, a fashion brand may buy leather directly from a leather consolidator and have it stitched in another country, such as Italy. That means your "Made in Italy" shoes might be made with leather from a Bangladeshi tannery.

What Companies Can Do when Abusive Conditions Are Discovered

Imagine reading a headline about one of your favorite brands that is accused of labor abuse in its supply chain or sexual misconduct by a senior executive. Do you drop the brand abruptly or wait to see whether the company turns around the situation?

Some companies have strong due diligence processes and transparently report misconduct or abuse in their own supply chains.[47] For example, in 2021, chocolate company Tony's Chocolonely started working with two new cocoa farms in West Africa and found 1,700 cases of child labor.[48] As a result, Tony's Chocolonely now works with the cocoa farms to solve the problems and is committed to reporting its actions and findings. Those 1,700 kids now have a chance to go to school and play.

However, most companies aren't aware that there's sexual harassment or labor abuse going on, especially in their complex supply chains.[49] After all, these behaviors are illegal and thus hidden in the shadows. Investigations bring light to these dark places. Some investigations are private while others, such as the 2023 *New York Times* investigation of child labor in the United States, are made public.

Once an investigation has brought the issues to light, companies can respond. The companies mentioned in the *New York Times* for having child labor in their supply chains claimed they would invest in improving auditing of suppliers. Improved audits theoretically help prevent suppliers' use of child labor.

When a company discovers abusive labor conditions in its supply chains, it has three options:

1. Stop using the product or ingredient.
2. Change to an ethical supplier.
3. Continue to source from problematic factories and work toward long-lasting solutions.

Ask yourself: *Do I want to support companies that address the problems—despite some concerns about their immediate impact? Or do I prefer to buy from companies that have taken a stance and moved their business or innovated to no longer require the problematic product or ingredient?*

Mica is a good example. It's a mineral commonly used in cosmetics to add shimmer and can be found in lipstick, eyeshadow, nail polish, sunscreen, and more. Current trends in makeup include lots of glitter, and glitter means mica. The demand for shimmery makeup is expected to grow steadily over the next five years.[50] Unfortunately, much of the world's mica has an ingrained human rights issue along with its shimmer. A quarter of the world's mica comes from small, dangerous, and illegal mines in Jharkhand and Bihar, India, where child labor is widespread.[51] Child labor in mica mines is also prevalent in Brazil, China, Madagascar, Peru, Pakistan, and Sri Lanka.[52]

Companies such as Estée Lauder and L'Oréal joined with the human rights nonprofit organization Terres des Hommes to form the Responsible Mica Initiative (RMI),[53] which now has almost sixty members. Critics of the RMI say its efforts are insufficient given the gravity of the child labor issue. Other critics simply ask, why use mica when alternatives are available that do not require mining?

If you are uncertain if a product contains mica, you can contact the company via its website's Contact Us tab and ask. Let them know that you don't want to wear mica mined by children. If you don't hear back, consider switching brands. See Tip #5 below for how to contact brands.

At the time of this writing, only two brands—Dr. Hauschka and Odylique—use Fair Trade Certified ingredients.

ALL EMPLOYEES DESERVE FAIR TREATMENT

How do your favorite brands treat their own employees? Most employees of American brands are based in the United States and are protected by minimum wage, health and safety standards, and other regulations. Yet many U.S. workers do not benefit from the high level of standards we expect. From butchers to cooks in chain restaurants, retail workers, and delivery teams, many people who make and sell products work in tough and sometimes unsafe environments. To understand how a brand treats its own employees, I look at a company's stance on unions and diversity as key indicators. These are not perfect proxies but they are somewhat indicative.

Unions

Does the company allow freedom of association, which is a fancy way of saying, does it allow unions? Unions can help secure high-quality health and safety standards, as well as fair pay. A labor union negotiates collectively with an employer to protect and further workers' rights and interests. A resurgence in unions was sparked during the COVID-19 pandemic to help ensure that workers had protective gear, sick pay, and protection from mass layoffs.[54]

Diversity, Equity, and Inclusion (DEI)

Equal opportunity, pay equity, and nondiscrimination also remain challenges for many employees. Gender equality and LGBTQ+ nondiscrimination need to be components of any company's principles.

I often look at the number of women, racial minorities and LGBTQ+ people working as senior executives or on the company's board as an indicator of that firm's general diversity. Why? A company's culture and policies are traditionally created via a top-down approach. How the top ranks of a company are structured will typically be replicated throughout the company. A diverse senior leadership team helps to ensure fair and supportive policies and an understanding that supports equitable opportunities. This isn't just feel-good—it's smart business to gain diverse insights and viewpoints.

YOUR SHOPPING SUPERPOWER TIPS AND TOOLS

Now that you've got the backstory, it's time to respond by making some product switches you can feel good about. You'll signal to your favorite brands that you want products made with fair labor conditions. For example, I recently bought a Godiva chocolate bar. Delicious. Fruity and not too sweet. I'd never bought Godiva before and didn't know anything about the brand. I looked it up on the 2024 Chocolate Score Card, a rating system based on social and environmental criteria. Godiva scored poorly across the range of indicators, including fair wages. I decided that, despite its great taste, I would stop buying this brand. Now I choose chocolates that rank at the top of the score card.

With good information, you can make better shopping choices. The goal is for you to quickly find the information you need. Sometimes it will be good news, and you'll learn that the brands you like match your expectations and values. But sometimes the information will cause you to stop and think, as it did me with the Godiva chocolate. No brand is perfect, and you can't know everything about how workers are treated. The goal is to make informed choices, based on what you can learn from trusted sources. Pursue progress, not perfection.

This section covers the following tips and tools on how to

- Make one impactful change a week.
- Seek trustworthy certifications.
- Use rating systems, directories, and apps.
- Avoid the worst offenders.
- Tell the brands you care.

You'll find a summary for easy decision-making at the end of the chapter. Each of the following chapters offers the same types of tips for planet, community, and health.

Tip #1: Make One Impactful Change a Week

Make it your goal to reconsider one product a week. Consider your options and then choose a brand that aligns more closely with your values. Make changes that have impact. Put your energy and money where it matters most and focus on products that have high risks of labor abuse.

Start by investigating one product a week that you buy routinely, such as coffee, tea, or chocolate. After a few weeks, switch to a product for something you buy less often—such as gifts, clothes, or toys. With this approach, you'll slowly change your shopping habits for good.

Routine Purchases to Switch for Impact

The following are household staples with high risk of labor abuse, below subsistence pay rates, and child and slave labor:

- *Coffee and tea:* Almost half of all coffee and tea smallholder farmers and plantation workers often face poverty due to the low prices paid for their crops and low wages.[55, 56] Programs such as Fair Trade and Fair for Life and many small coffee brands such as Equal Exchange that buy directly from farmers pay a premium so that farmers earn a "fair" price to assist them on the route out of poverty. These types of programs make up about 6 to 8 percent of all coffee production, so your purchase can help fair coffee grow to 10 percent of the total market. A 10 percent market share will clearly demonstrate to the big brands that they can—and need to—address the working conditions of their coffee suppliers.

- *Chocolate:* Imagine a child climbing a tree. Now imagine that this child is holding a sharp machete, climbing out onto a thin branch, and cutting cocoa bean pods. The child does this work for up to fourteen hours a day. Once they cut the bean pods from the trees, the child packs the pods into hundred -pound sacks and carries them through the forest.[57] This is the daily reality for about 2 million children in West Africa who work in cocoa farming.

The six largest chocolate companies—Hershey, Mars, Nestlé, Mondelēz, Ferrara, and Meiji—source about 80 percent of the world's chocolate, most of which comes from West Africa. Eradicating child labor is difficult. Despite efforts by many brands, recent research shows there are more child laborers in West African cocoa plantations in 2023 than there were in 2010,[58] when the problem was first acknowledged and companies were forced to act.

- *Bananas*: Child labor, exposure to aerial-sprayed toxic pesticides, and human rights abuses are commonly found in banana plantations in Central and South America, which is the source of most bananas eaten in the United States.

- *Sugar*: Hand-harvested cane sugar has high risks of slavery and labor abuse. Sugar is sold as a commodity, which means sugar from multiple sources is mixed together. Only sugar from a distinct supply chain, such as sugar that is certified as fair labor, organic, or Bonsucro—a sustainability standard— can be verified. Since North American beet sugar is mechanically harvested, it doesn't have labor issues.

- *Fish and seafood*: Much of the fish eaten in the United States is caught in the Pacific Ocean by trawlers in international waters. Some of the trawling boats in Asia and Africa operate covert slave labor rings and perpetrate horrific abuses. Ships often transfer their catch to and from other vessels, allowing fishing boats to remain at sea for years at a time, with workers trapped. Similarly, some shrimp production is tainted by labor abuse. In Thailand and India, migrant laborers are trafficked into slavery to work the shrimp farms.

Most of the canned tuna eaten in the United States comes from Thailand, Ecuador, and China. According to the International Labor Office, workers from poor regions across Asia have been trafficked to work in fish canning in Thailand, and labor abuse is suspected to be common in other countries.

The country of origin is listed on fresh or packaged fish, so you can avoid fish and seafood from high-risk countries. However, canned fish seldom states the country of origin or canning location. The industry has taken steps to meet international labor and environmental standards through the Seafood Task Force.[59] Look on the task force's website for participating brands. An alternative is to buy dolphin-friendly canned fish directly from small fisheries in the Pacific Northwest.

Occasional Purchases to Switch for Impact

You probably know in advance that you need to pick up a gift or get a new pair of jeans, so there's time to spend a few minutes looking for a well-sourced item. Common yet infrequent purchases that often have a high risk of labor abuse and poverty pay rates include the following:

- fashion: clothing, shoes, accessories
- rugs and soft home furnishings
- cosmetics
- leather goods
- gold and other jewelry

For these purchases, you have two options. You can buy locally made goods, which are generally a safe bet because the artisan usually takes care with sourcing. You'll find tips on how to find locally made goods in Chapter 6. Or you can buy from brands that work to ensure all workers in their supply chains are treated fairly. The following tips will help you find trustworthy brands, and guidelines are summarized at the end of the chapter.

Tip #2: Trustworthy Certifications

The list below covers robust and frequently used third-party certification programs for ingredients, products, and brands. Look for these certifications. As explained in Chapter 3, company standards are often weaker than third-party certification standards, and it's often impossible to tell what is real and what is a bogus marketing ploy.

Third-Party Independent Certification Marks

Fair Trade Certified is the most common mark and has become synonymous with fair labor practices. It is trustworthy and robust and covers different types of ingredients, products, and brands. But don't overlook the other fair labor certifications.

FAIR TRADE CERTIFIED™

Fair Trade Certifications

Fair Trade has two marks: Fair Trade Certified—which you're more likely to see— and Fairtrade International. Run by different but related organizations, they stand for the same values and ensure that a living wage is paid to workers. The workers' communities also receive a lump sum to invest as they wish, be it for schools or healthcare centers. Both fair trade groups certify products as well as ingredients, which means that a food product may contain some fair trade ingredients, such as sugar or cocoa, along with conventional ingredients.

What products are certified? Thousands of products and ingredients are certified, including food, clothing, beauty products, flowers, vitamins, shoes, and home goods.

Where will you find this label? Look for a wide range of products in your grocery store—from soap to coconuts, baking mixes to sugar. I often use the Fair Trade Certified online shopping guide to find brands and products. You'll find Fair Trade Certified drinks and food at some cafes and restaurants. Certified apparel is sold online and at major retailers. For example, Madewell and Target sell Fair Trade Certified denim. Cotopaxi, REI, Patagonia, Madewell, prAna, and Eileen Fisher offer a growing range of Fair Trade Certified options. I recently bought Fair Trade Certified knitting wool online from Purl Soho.

Fair for Life

This product certification indicates that producers and workers earn a fair wage and have safe working conditions. Environmental sustainability is part of these standards. The Fair for Life process monitors fair trade projects to ensure that their impact improves over time.

What products are certified? Products made from natural raw materials. Some Fair for Life products are also certified organic.

Where will you find this label? There are more than 500 certified Fair for Life products including fruit, vegetables, almonds, aloe vera, tea, rice, soaps and shampoos, chocolate, spices, coconut oil, honey, shea butter, wine, and more. You'll find this label on Theo Chocolate and Dr. Bronner's Soap, among others.

Rainforest Alliance (RA) Green Frog

RA's Green Frog seal encourages farmers to adopt sustainable agriculture practices to produce better quality, more sustainable, and climate-resilient crops, which enable farmers to reduce costs, increase their productivity over time, and ultimately improve their livelihoods. The standards prohibit the use of forced labor, child labor, and discrimination, and require that farmers have the right to organize. This is a great certification because it combines sustainable development, fair wages, and environmental concerns.

What products are certified? Cocoa, coffee, flowers and plants, fruits, herbs, spices, nuts, tea, and vegetables.

Where will you find this label? Grocery stores, online, and RA's product guide.

GoodWeave

Handwoven rugs are often made with child labor. The GoodWeave label ensures that no child or forced labor is used in the making of a certified product, and that your purchase supports programs that educate children and ensure decent work for adults. Focused initially in India and Pakistan, GoodWeave now works globally. During its twenty-five years of on-the-ground work, GoodWeave has rescued about 9,000 children from slavery and helped almost 50,000 go to school.

What products are certified? Individual rugs, soft home furnishings.

Where will you find this label? On the rug or home furnishing. You'll find GoodWeave rugs at Target, Macy's, The Rug Company, and many other home furnishing stores. Check the GoodWeave website for a comprehensive list.

Nest

Nest is an important breakthrough program that ensures that ethical working standards apply to artisan work and handwork contracted to be done at home. This type of at-home work is usually hidden under layers of subcontracting agreements, since home workers are dispersed throughout cities and rural communities. Home workers are often vulnerable to abuse, with forced overtime to meet quotas and exposure to toxic glues and dyes. Nest's Ethical Handcraft program currently works in over thirty-four countries, with more than 165 artisan businesses and over 210,000 handworkers.

What products are certified? Handmade goods such as home décor, apparel, accessories, and furniture.

Where will you find this label? West Elm, Patagonia, Target, Pottery Barn, Madewell, and other brands are pioneering this certification program and championing standards for at-home work. Check Nest's website for the growing list.

Certification Marks That Cover Brands and Companies

Butterfly Mark

Love luxury and quality craftsmanship? Look for the Butterfly Mark for trustworthy information about a brand's social and environmental performance. The mark is awarded to entire brands, not specific products. The certification covers twenty-three topics across four key pillars: labor standards; diversity, equality, and inclusion; community involvement; and social responsibility throughout the supply chain. It also covers environmental performance, governance topics, and sustainable innovation.

What products are certified? About 200 brands are certified, including products in the following industries: fashion, travel, interiors, premium drinks, jewelry and watches, and beauty and fragrance products.

Where will you find this label? Brand websites, as well as some retailers' sites. Some products carry the Butterfly Mark on their tags and other packaging. The Connected Butterfly Mark Digital Brand Passport gives you easy access to luxury brands' performance details and ratings.

B Corporations (B Corps)

B Corps are for-profit companies that are driven by both mission and profit. The companies meet a range of stringent environmental and social performance criteria and give back to local communities. The certification is verified by B Labs, a global nonprofit. It's a safe bet that any product from a B Corp is a good match if you value the fair treatment of workers.

What companies are certified B Corps? B Corps come in all sizes, from multinational companies to one-person start-ups. About 4,000 companies are registered B Corps. A few of the most well-known are Patagonia, Ben & Jerry's, Allbirds, Tom's, Warby Parker, Bombas, and Athleta. Two of my favorite online shops for gifts—Uncommon Goods and Prosperity Candles—are B Corps.

Where will you find this label? You'll see the B Corp logo on the front page of websites and sometimes on products.

U.S. Cotton Trust Protocol

This is a voluntary sustainability program and traceability platform for U.S. cotton. If you want to ensure that you're purchasing cotton that was produced with fair labor, buying garments with this logo or hangtag is a good option.

What companies use this protocol? Millers, manufacturers, and brands such as Levi's, Ralph Lauren, and The Gap.

Where will you find this label? On hangtags and labels of garments sold by participating brands. Check the U.S. Cotton Trust Protocol website for a full list of participating brands.

World Fair Trade Organization (WFTO)

The WFTO verifies enterprises that fully practice fair trade in eighty-four countries, with more than 1 million livelihoods impacted globally. Almost three-quarters of the affected people are women.

The WFTO Guarantee System ensures that businesses maintain the highest standards of sustainability, encompassing both environmental and social aspects.

What products are verified? Fashion to houseware, food, and beauty products.

Where will you find this label? The WFTO website connects businesses with certified suppliers. Look for specialized gift shops, such as refugee-made products sold at Made51.org. See Chapter 6 for more about refugee-made products.

Equal Exchange

Equal Exchange is not a certification system but it deserves mention. A worker-owned fair trade and organic company, Equal Exchange has been a leader in the fair trade movement since the 1980s. It trades with small farmer co-ops and associations, manufactures coffee and tea, and sells products from small family farms.

What products are produced? Coffee and tea, almonds, dried fruits and nuts, spices, and condiments from small family farms.

Where will you find this label? Grocery stores, specialty stores, and online.

Industry Collaborations

Many companies work together to tackle difficult issues rather than certifying their products. Check if a company participates in industry-wide collaborative programs with clear standards and third-party verification or audits. The main programs that indicate the brand is making progress in workers' rights include the following:

- Responsible Jewelry
- Responsible Mica Initiative
- Responsible Toys
- Better Cotton Initiative
- Better Sugar Initiative
- Better Factories Initiative

- Fair Labor Organization
- Better Work
- Amfori
- Nirapon
- The International Accord

Tip #3: Rating Systems, Directories, and Apps

Ratings and rankings make it easy to assess whether your favorite brand aligns with your values. Ratings are run by independent, usually not-for-profit groups that rate brands and products based on their social performance. Good rating and ranking systems rely on rigorous, verified data and fact-checking. Some are app based, others web based. All of those listed are free to use except Ethical Consumer, which is a paid subscription service.

Below are a few of my favorites, listed by types of products they cover: fashion, chocolate, and lifestyle.

Fashion, Apparel, and Footwear

Remake: Remake is a global nonprofit fighting for human rights and climate justice in the clothing industry. Its annual *Fashion Accountability Report* rates fashion brands by measuring their supply chains' performance on human rights, environmental, economic, and political issues. Brands are scored based on their behavior and actual progress, not just on what they say they are going to do. To amplify the impact, Remake contacts each company assessed to discuss how the brand can adopt more sustainable practices. You may be surprised how some of your favorite brands rank. The organization does not accept funding from fashion companies.

Remake's #PayUp Campaign: If you think brands should honor contracts to ensure garment workers are paid fairly, check out the #PayUp campaign. When a company breaks a contract and cancels orders, it often leads to nonpayment of wages or unemployment—or both—among the most vulnerable women workers in the garment industry. Remake tracks companies on the role they play in issues concerning garment workers' rights, including whether the companies honored contracts without delays in payments or discounts during the pandemic. For example, PVH Corps—which owns the Calvin Klein and Tommy Hilfiger brands—was among the first targeted companies to reverse its decision to cancel orders during the pandemic and paid garment workers in full.[60]

Good On You App: This app uses a five-star rating system to rank fashion brands. Since 2015, Good On You has assessed more than 3,000 brands, including shoes, sleepwear, and fashion. Enter the brand name of a garment, and a score appears with a brief explanation. Is your favorite brand not covered? You can suggest it. And if a brand ranks poorly, the app helps you send a quick note to ask a question or urge the company to do better.

Renoon: Renoon's app helps you discover brands from multiple online shops that match Renoon's sustainability criteria, which combine workers' rights and environmental concerns. Companies pay Renoon to help increase their transparency and communicate with customers.

Chocolate

The Chocolate Score Card: This is my go-to rating for chocolate. It ranks a chocolate company's performance on key sustainability issues, including human rights, living income, child labor, deforestation, and climate. Five nonprofits created the system, which is based on rigorous academic research.[61] The companies range from the largest cocoa traders and chocolate manufacturers in the industry, such as Cargil and Nestlé, to smaller, innovative companies, such as Tony's Chocolonely and Alter Eco. The scores are updated annually, usually just in time for Easter.

LeafScore is an independent "ethical" rater of a range of products. Its review of chocolate covers labor, deforestation, and palm oil. LeafScore provides its top five picks and offers a few additional good options. Its criteria differ from the Chocolate Score Card, so it adds good choices to your chocolate list.

Lifestyle and Other Goods

Buycott: A clever alternative to boycotts, Buycott helps you buy from responsible companies. It personalizes product ratings based on what matters most to you and how strongly you feel about the issues. Buycott covers a range of products, from fashion to fruit. When you come across a product you want to investigate, scan the product's barcode with your phone, and the app will tell you whether there's a clash with any of your values. It will also inform you of any other controversies concerning the brand. Plus, like the Good On You app, it enables you to send a message to the brand telling them why you won't buy their product.

DoneGood app and Web Extension: This app can help you discover products that are built to last—and brands that work to reduce poverty and fight climate change. Enter the kind of product that you're looking for and the app will list companies that are "doing good" in respect to the issues you've listed. DoneGood also provides shoppers discount codes for companies doing social good.

Ethical Consumer: This paid subscription service creates personalized product guides that reflect the issues that are most important to you. Covering everything from canned food to travel insurance, the service takes your top areas of concerns and then ranks products accordingly. The service covers sweatshop labor, climate, genetically modified crops, palm oil, deforestation, and more. The site ranks the parent company behind the brand, not just the brand. For example, it ranks PVH Corp., not Calvin Klein. It also enables you to e-mail or post about a company to let them know that you will (or won't) be buying their products.

Tip #4: Avoid the Worst Offenders

Sometimes avoiding the worst is the best you can do. This means avoiding any products that might be tainted with slavery and abusive child labor.

Slavery and child labor are most frequently found in farming, mining, and fishing. Slaves have been found picking fruit and tomatoes in the United States and Mexico, tuna fishing for Thai canning companies, and stitching apparel in Brazil. Unfortunately, the "Made in" label tells only a part of a product's story. For finished products such as cotton clothing, they do not stipulate the source of the raw material.[62] You can't know if cotton comes, for example, from Kazakhstan, a country with a track record of forced child labor in cotton fields.

However, you can take steps to avoid the worst. Table 4.1 lists ingredients and finished products that have the highest risk of slave labor if they are sourced from the listed countries.[63] The third column lists what to buy to avoid the worst practices.

Table 4.1. Products to Avoid from High Risk Countries

Product	Source Countries with High Risk of Slavery and Child Labor	What to Buy to Avoid Slavery and Child Labor
Beef	Brazil, Bolivia, Niger, Paraguay	U.S. beef or certified from other countries, or certified organic
Cocoa	Ivory Coast, Nigeria	Companies highly ranked on the Chocolate Score Card "Bean to bar" makers who buy directly from cocoa producers in other countries
Coffee	Brazil, Ivory Coast	Fair Trade Certified or similar, including organic or farm-direct single-source coffee
Cotton	Benin, Burkina Faso, India, Kazakhstan, Pakistan, Tajikistan, Turkmenistan, China	Fair Trade Certified or similar, including organic North American-, European-, Egyptian-grown cotton and garments with U.S. Cotton Trust Protocol certification
Electronics	China, Malaysia	Buy from companies with a track record of addressing labor abuses.
Fish	Bangladesh (dried fish), China, Ghana (tilapia), Indonesia, Taiwan, Thailand (tuna, shrimp)	Certified Marine Stewardship Council (MSC) fish and seafood, or at least fish from other countries
Garments and Textiles	Argentina, Brazil, China, Ethiopia, India, Malaysia, Nepal (carpets), Pakistan (carpets), Thailand, Vietnam	For carpets: GoodWeave, Fair Trade Certified, or Butterfly Mark For clothes: Investigate what the brand is doing to ensure safe labor conditions.
Gold and Diamonds	Ivory Coast, Angola, Sierra Leone, Liberia, Central African Republic, Democratic Republic of Congo	Conflict-free gold and diamonds: Look for Responsible Jewelry Coalition (RJC) certification at the company level.

Table 4.1. Products to Avoid from High Risk Countries (Continued)

Product	Source Countries with High Risk of Slavery and Child Labor	What to Buy to Avoid Slavery and Child Labor
Mica	India	Products with no natural mica or companies in the Responsible Mica Initiative
Rice	Burma, India, Mali	Check country of origin. Buy organic, Fair Life, or Fair Trade Certified.
Rubber Gloves	Malaysia, China	Fair trade natural latex gloves from responsibly managed rubber tree plantations and factories
Sugarcane	Bolivia, Dominican Republic, Brazil, Pakistan	Fair Trade Certified or similar, including organic. Beet sugar from North America or with Bonsucro accreditation
Tomato Products	China	Tomatoes from China's Xinjiang province are banned from import into the United States.
Yarn	China	Fair Trade Certified or similar, organic, or sourced from another country

Tip #5: Tell the Brand You Care

Communicating with the brand is one of the easiest and most impactful things you can do. Brands are sensitive to what their consumers say. For example, in 2022 Remake led a group of concerned shoppers to flood the inbox of Victoria's Secret to demand they pay legally owed compensation to workers in Thailand. Within a year, Victoria's Secret paid $8.3 million to more than 1,250 Thai workers who sewed bras for the company.[64]

Find the contact e-mail address on the brand's website and send a brief and specific message. To start your note, let the brand know that you are already a loyal customer, a first-time buyer, or considering switching to their brand: "I'm a fan of your brand, and I care about how workers are treated in your supply chains."

Next, share your concerns and be as specific as possible. For example:

- If you are concerned about worker safety in factories, ask, "How do you ensure that factory workers making your [shirts, toys, furniture, canned tuna] are working in a safe environment?"

- If you are concerned about child and forced labor, ask, "What are you doing to ensure that no child labor or forced labor is used anywhere in your supply chains, particularly in [mica, canned fish, sugarcane, etc.]?"

- If you want to ensure workers are paid a fair wage, ask, "Have you considered ensuring that a living wage is paid to all workers in your supply chain? I think it's only fair that everyone can afford the basics, and I want to buy brands that support fair labor practices."

- If you want to support diversity and women's leadership within companies, ask, "Do you have any specific goals to increase the number of women on your board? How representative is your senior leadership in terms of gender and diversity?"

Next, state what you want them to do. Tell them no more blue-washing, unfair labor practices, or high-risk labor markets. Make it clear what is at stake. If nothing changes, will you stop purchasing the product and switch to a competitor? Will you share your actions and reasons with friends or on social media?

SUMMING IT UP

Focus on one change a week. Keep going. As your changes build over time, so will your confidence and contentment with what you buy.

Buy products that

- have third-party certification
- rank well in rigorous ratings and assessments
- are made by local artisans
- are made by companies you've come to know and trust

Table 4.2. High-Impact Switches for Frequent Purchases

Product	Prioritize Buying
Bananas	Fair Trade Certified or other certification, including organic
Chocolate	Top-scoring companies on Chocolate Score Card or LeafScore, certified Fair Trade Certified, Equal Exchange, Fair for Life, or other certifications, including organic; "bean to bar" makers that buy directly from cocoa producers
Coffee and Tea	Fair Trade Certified or other similar certifications, including organic or small-batch "direct from farmer" coffee roasters
Fish and Seafood	Frozen, fresh, or canned fish and seafood from North America and Europe, or fish with Marine Stewardship Council (MSC) certification
Household Products	Rainforest Alliance, Fair Trade Certified, Fair for Life, similar certifications including organic; see Chapter 7 on health aspects
Other Food and Drinks	Rainforest Alliance, Fair Trade Certified, Equal Exchange, Fair for Life, B Corps, Marine Stewardship Council, certified organic, locally grown and produced
Sugar	Fair labor certified sugar such as Fair Trade Certified or Equal Exchange, beet sugar from North America, or organic cane sugar; sugar from companies with Bonsucro accreditation

Table 4.3. High-Impact Switches for Special-Occasion and Infrequent Purchases

Product	Prioritize Buying Products with Certifications or from Brands That Collaborate to Solve Issues or Rank Well in Ratings
Cosmetics	Fair Trade ingredients, no natural mica, Responsible Mica Initiative; ranks well on Environmental Working Group, Ethical Consumer
Fashion: Clothes, Shoes, and Accessories	Fair Trade Certifications, Butterfly Mark, B Corp, or similar; participates in Remake campaigns or other programs such as Better Factories.; ranks well on Good On You, Done Good, Pay Up, Renoon, Ethical Consumer
Gifts	Nest, Butterfly Mark, Fair Trade Certified, B Corps, WFTO, similar certifications; ranks well on Buycott, Ethical Consumer, Done Good
Handmade Items	Nest, Fair Trade Certified, Fair for Life, WFTO, similar certifications; ranks well on Buycott, Ethical Consumer, Done Good, etc.
Jewelry, Gold, and Watches	Butterfly Mark, Nest, WFTO, or member of the Responsible Jewelry Coalition; gold and gems from North America
Leather Goods	Butterfly Mark or Nest certified, Leather Working Group; materials sourced from North America or Europe
Resorts, Travel	Butterfly Mark; member, Select Green Hotels; ranks well on Responsible Travel (UK)
Rugs and Soft Furnishings	GoodWeave, Nest, Fair Trade, similar certifications; ranks well on Buycott, Ethical Consumer, Done Good, etc.
Toys	Member, Responsible Toy Initiative; ranks well on Buycott, Ethical Consumer, Done Good, etc.

Chapter 5

PLANET: BUY ENVIRONMENTALLY RESPONSIBLE PRODUCTS

All products originate from natural resources. A plastic bottle began as crude oil, a rayon shirt as wood pulp. Everything we use originated from Earth's materials. Natural resources depend on healthy ecological systems to generate timber, food, minerals, fuels, and other essential materials.

Consider what it takes to make a simple product such as pasta: land, water, and soil nutrients for the wheat; energy to harvest and transform the grain into spaghetti; tree pulp for the cardboard packaging; and fuel to ship, distribute, and dispose of the package.

Some products are made in ways that deplete natural resources unnecessarily or cause irreparable damage to ecological systems. For instance, an efficient cotton textile factory with water-saving technologies may use as little as 20 to 83 liters of water to produce a kilogram of knit fabric, whereas an inefficient factory requires up to 377 liters of water per kilogram.[65] Many products that contain palm oil could find alternative formulations. Producing palm oil causes extensive deforestation and destruction of rainforests in Southeast Asia, endangering species such as orangutans and causing irreversible biodiversity loss.

Other products are made in ways that respect the planet, even helping to restore it. For example, closed-loop manufacturing focuses on recycling and reusing materials to create a self-sustaining cycle. It minimizes waste, reduces the need for new raw materials, and greatly decreases overall waste production. Regenerative farming can restore pastureland and improve soil biomes.

No single measurement captures the environmental impact of a brand or a product because ecological systems are interlocking and interdependent. Unintended consequences send ripples through the environment: A table or chair made from unsustainable tropical wood causes deforestation, which in turn harms biodiversity and aggravates climate change by reducing carbon sequestration. Many of the impacts occur far from us, often seemingly invisibly.

In this chapter, you'll learn

- how to identify which products are made with care for the environment and its core systems
- which products are particularly damaging and should be avoided

FIVE SYSTEMS

The Earth's systems are supported by interrelated biophysical processes. The four most impacted by what we buy are climate, biodiversity, land use, and water. Waste is a major source of environmental damage, so I add it here as a fifth system. This section provides a high-level overview of the five systems so that you can choose where to focus your initial shopping changes.

Climate

What we buy and consume in our households causes up to 60 percent of greenhouse gases.[66] That's a sobering statistic. It's much easier to think of climate change being driven by someone else, "over there." What we buy matters because manufacturing, raising cattle, other forms of agriculture, the fashion industry, overfishing, and global shipping are significant drivers of climate change.[67]

Take plastics. Under the status quo, plastics are expected in fifteen years to account for almost 20 percent of total greenhouse gases.[68] Almost half of all plastics are single-use.[69] Can you see how the impact of single-use plastic bags, food containers, and packaging adds up?

Climate scientists around the world agree that the world's average temperature should not rise more than 1.5 degrees Celsius (2.7 degrees Fahrenheit) above preindustrial levels. Exceeding this threshold, as the world did in 2024, is expected to lead to worsening and potentially irreversible effects. Reducing carbon and other greenhouse gas emissions by 40 percent by 2030 is necessary to avoid more severe climate change impacts, according to the climate agreement signed by 196 countries and the European Union in Paris in 2015.[70] That is a tall order.

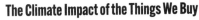

The Climate Impact of the Things We Buy

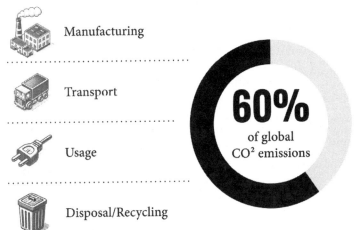

Manufacturing

Transport

Usage

Disposal/Recycling

60%
of global
CO^2 emissions

Biodiversity

When we lose a species, it's gone forever. Biodiversity includes both the variety and variability of life on Earth, encompassing variations at the genetic, species, and ecosystem levels. The main drivers of biodiversity loss are deforestation, overfishing, agriculture, climate change, invasive species, urbanization, and pollution.

Wildlife is at risk globally. Average wildlife populations have declined more than 70 percent in just fifty years, according to the World Wide Fund for Nature's Living Planet Report 2024.

Biodiversity matters because it helps ecosystems function smoothly and adapt to change. Think of the humble bee or another pollinating insect. Pollinators are essential for agriculture because they help the reproduction of many crops by transferring pollen, which enables fruit and seed production. Additionally, pollinators help maintain biodiversity by supporting the growth of wild plants, which provide habitats and food sources for various wildlife species. Pollinators, including bees, are increasingly endangered by the widespread use of pesticides, which can directly kill pollinators or alter behaviors such as navigation and reproduction, leading to population declines.

Modern agriculture and food production rely on a narrow spectrum of genetic diversity, driving the loss of old cultivars and varieties. Yet plant genetic diversity helps farmers around the world respond to crop diseases and ensures resilience in the face of climate or water stress.

When plants are genetically similar, they become highly susceptible to diseases and pests. If a disease or pest emerges, it can rapidly spread and devastate entire crops across large regions because there is no genetic variation to provide resistance. One of the worst famines in human history began in 1845 in Ireland when a mold killed potato plants. The lack of genetic variation in Irish potatoes enabled the disease to spread rapidly.

Take bananas. More than 500 banana varieties are grown around the world. Yet each year more and more local varieties are replaced with a single high-yielding dessert banana variety, the Cavendish. More than 47 percent of all bananas grown worldwide are now Cavendish, including those you find in your grocery store.

Diverse plant and animal species are also the basis of many modern pharmaceutical drugs that help treat cancer, heart disease, and illnesses such as malaria. Biodiversity loss could mean losing potential future treatments for disease.

Land-based species are not the only ones impacted. Overfishing and bycatch from commercial fisheries harm biodiversity. Bycatch includes anything a fishing crew catches in its nets that isn't the target fish species, including dolphins, turtles, and other marine mammals. Catchall nets aren't necessary, and pole fishing eliminates bycatch.

Some species are threatened by overfishing, leading to a depletion of fish stocks that imperil the broader ocean ecosystem.

Biodiversity loss puts livelihoods and cultural traditions at risk. For example overfishing imperils the livelihoods of traditional lobstering and fishing communities along U.S. coastlines. Another example is the monarch butterfly's migration, which has greatly diminished in the last fifteen years. Revered for centuries by Indigenous communities in Mexico, such as the Nahua, Otomi, and Purepecha peoples, the arrival of the butterflies in the Oyamel fir forests of Central Mexico is considered a spiritual event, symbolizing the return of the souls of departed ancestors and the renewal of life. The decline in monarchs has sparked conservation efforts, including reforesting parts of Central Mexico because communities cherish the symbolism and inspiration of the butterflies.

Hamburgers, Deforestation, and Climate Change

Cattle production remains the top cause of deforestation in Brazil and other countries. Land is cleared to raise cattle, which are fed soy that's been planted on cleared land. Cattle belch methane gas, which causes twenty-eight times more global warming than carbon dioxide. Cattle, with all that belching, contribute to nearly 6 percent of total greenhouse gas emissions.[71]

Cattle mean hamburgers, and lots of them. McDonald's is the world's largest hamburger chain, with more than 30,000 restaurants. After years of pressure from environmental activists, McDonald's committed in 2017 to eliminating deforestation from its global supply chains by 2030.[72] Its deforestation commitment applies to all its beef, fiber-based packaging, coffee, palm oil, and poultry. In 2023, McDonald's claimed that nearly all beef and chicken used by the company is sourced from suppliers who do not engage in deforestation, including for feed. This comes a few years ahead of European Union regulations that will require full transparency about potential sources of deforestation from imported products such as beef and chicken.

What's hidden in your burger?

Land Use

How land is managed affects climate, biodiversity, and waterways. For example, soil can be damaged by overuse and overgrazing, heavy applications of agrochemicals, erosion, floods, and growing the same crop year after year on the same land. Depleted soil can't grow food. Soil health is the unsexy linchpin of a healthy planet.

Converting wilderness by clearing it for development is a double whammy. Both cutting forests and clearing land cause carbon emissions. Forests act as the lungs of the planet, helping to regulate carbon. If the planet loses forests, it loses lung capacity. Almost 90 percent of deforestation is caused by expanding agriculture, including pasture cattle, soy production for livestock feed, palm oil plantations,[73] and certain commodity crops such as coffee.

In Indonesia, Malaysia and other Asian countries, Central and South America, and increasingly in Central and West Africa, forests are cut down for palm oil plantations. Palm oil is the world's most used and globally traded vegetable oil. It goes into everything from soap to peanut butter to ice cream. Land clearing for palm oil plantations leads to widespread rainforest destruction, peatland degradation, and devastating wildlife loss.[74]

Bad News and Good News About Palm Oil

Palm oil bought by Americans between 2021 and 2023 is estimated to have provoked more than 100,000 acres of deforestation, mostly in Indonesia.[75] That's an area larger than Yellowstone National Park. The estimate does not include imports of manufactured products, such as chocolate and cosmetics, that contain palm oil.

Most food conglomerates that rely on palm oil—including General Mills, Kellogg's, Nestlé, and Mondelēz—have commitments to ensure that they use only sustainable palm oil. However, according to the World Wide Fund for Nature (WWF) and the Rainforest Action Network (RAN) campaigning groups, many companies miss these targets.[76] Other environmentalists say that commercial palm oil can never be sustainable.

Despite the disheartening trends, research shows that the demand for sustainable palm oil by Western consumers and other factors led to an increase in sustainable production methods in Indonesia over the last decade.[77]

Water

A lot of water goes into making your stuff, and the world is short of fresh water.[78] In some countries, industry, manufacturing, and food production use as much as 40 percent of the country's fresh water. During the summer of 2024, more than 25 percent of the United States was in drought.[79] According to a study by the Columbia Water Center, many U.S. cities are at risk of water shortages, with varying levels of severity across different regions.[80]

The thirstiest industries are fruit and vegetables, textiles and garments, meat, beverages, and automotive. Top water polluters are tanneries, paper, chemicals, printing, and metal manufacturing. Some companies squander water, and many discharge contaminated wastewater into rivers and waterways.

Thirsty Jeans

Transforming cotton into denim and denim into your clothes takes a tremendous amount of water. Levi Strauss & Co., the company synonymous with jeans, decided to change this equation. In 2018, it set an ambitious goal to halve its cumulative water use for manufacturing in water-stressed areas by 2025. To do this, Levi Strauss & Co. transformed how denim is made by engaging almost everyone at the company, including engineers, designers, production staff, and sustainability experts. Not wanting to be the only skinny jeans at the party, Levi Strauss & Co. open-sourced its water-saving technology. Its technology is now used by many other apparel companies, including competitors.

Waste Management

If you're an average household in the United States, you recycle two out of ten recyclable items—and not all of that ends up recycled due to limited capacity at most municipal recycling facilities. Waste squanders resources, generates greenhouse gases, and increases poor and disadvantaged communities' risk of health problems. Landfilling waste can contribute to underground water pollution due to leaching and runoff, as well as to air pollution. Surprisingly, food waste contributes between 8 percent and 10 percent of total greenhouse gas emissions because it turns to methane.[81]

Plastic Exposure

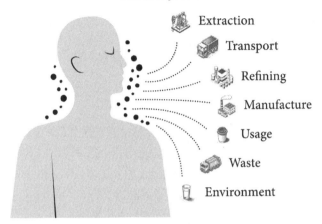

Part of the problem is that plastics don't break down; they break up. Over time, sun and heat turn plastics into increasingly smaller pieces until they become microscopic fragments. These microplastics are now just about everywhere on the planet: in the water, in fish, and in our bloodstreams.[82] A 2024 study found that the average American ingests five grams of plastic a week from food and plastic beverage and food containers. That is the equivalent of a credit card's worth of plastic consumed every week.[83]

What Happens to Your Unwanted Clothes?

- Less than 1 percent become recycled fibers turned into new clothes.
- More than 85 percent go to landfill or incineration, domestically or internationally.

- 8 percent is resold or exported for resale.
- 6 percent goes into industry rags, stuffing, and low-quality yarn or fabric made from the shredded fibers called shoddy.[84]

Returns? On average, shoppers return up to 30 percent of products bought online.[85] Most goods returned are not damaged, but many get destroyed anyway. If a seal has been broken or the packaging not perfectly intact, it's probably not going back to be sold by the original merchandiser. That means if you order shoes, open the box, try them on, and send them back, they will most likely not be resold by the retailer that sold them to you. A secondary market may pick up the item and resell it. However, many goods that are in perfect condition are sent to destroy-in-field companies that either landfill or incinerate them. Others are exported. Mountains of disposed fashion are exported to Latin America and Africa. About 60,000 tons of unwanted clothes arrive annually in Chile alone.[86] The immense volume of used clothes arriving in Chile, Ghana, Kenya, and other countries suppresses local clothing industries. Much of the secondhand clothes cannot be used, and tons of textiles are illegally dumped, creating environmental hazards and often combusting into uncontrolled fires.

Take one simple item—sneakers. About 300 million pairs of sneakers end up in landfills each year,[87] and most contain ethylene vinyl acetate that can last for as long as a thousand years in a landfill.[88]

The negative impact of convenient disposable packaging adds up. For example, according to the Environmental Protection Agency, U.S. consumers use about 25 billion polystyrene cups every year, 80

percent of which end up in the trash.[89] Once it's in a landfill, polystyrene takes about 500 years to break down.

About a third of all household waste is packaging.[90] Much of that
packaging is unrecyclable plastic, so it gets buried, burned, or littered.
If you want to reduce the waste generated from online shopping:

- Shop at brick-and-mortar shops, especially for items with a
  high likelihood of being sent back, such as shoes and clothing.
- Got an e-commerce return? Consider donating it to keep it
  from the landfill.
- If you must return items, use their original packaging.

Chemical waste is another concern, and it comes from many
sources. Thousands of variations of perfluoroalkyl and polyfluoroalkyl substances (PFAS) have been used for decades in food packaging, stain-resistant textiles, cookware, and home furnishings. They
are called "forever chemicals" because they don't break down. They
are known to be toxic to humans and are found in fish, in our food,
and in our blood.

You're exposed to PFAS in the products you buy—including
home furnishings, food packaging, and clothes—and from the industrial processes that make what you buy. (See Chapter 7 for PFAS
in clothing.) As shown below, PFAS also enter our drinking water
from industrial wastewater discharge. Change is slowly coming. In
2024, PFAS were banned in the United States for use in greaseproof
food packaging, commonly used in takeout food containers. Some
apparel companies also have stopped using PFAS.

How PFAS Gets into Your Air and Water

············· Air Emissions ·············

Industry   **Landfill**   **Farm** ···· Food ····▶ **Home**

Wastewater

Drinking water

Water Treatment   Fertilizers

Wastewater   Infiltration

Plant uptake

Rivers and Groundwater

HOW COMPANIES IMPACT THE ENVIRONMENT

Companies can significantly reduce their environmental impact in many ways, including by reducing greenhouse gas emissions, adopting climate goals, incorporating renewable energy sources into their production processes, optimizing resource efficiency, minimizing all waste, protecting biodiversity in their supply chains, reducing packaging, and innovating how and what the company produces. This is true for any company, whether it makes deodorant or canned peas.

At a minimum, a company needs to have a carbon reduction plan with time-bound goals.[91] It's a red flag if a large company has no publicly stated carbon reduction goals. Many companies have committed to switching to 100 percent renewable energy sources, in addition to tackling operational energy efficiency. Regulations in Europe and parts of the United States require companies to start reporting greenhouse gas emissions. This should nudge more companies into adopting reduction goals. See the Appendix for what to look for on a company's website about its environmental efforts.

Measuring and managing a company's impact on biodiversity are more complex than gauging carbon reduction. Today there is no easy way to tell if a company is making efforts to protect biodiversity, but this will change soon. In the next few years, companies will begin to report their impact on natural resources, including biodiversity, which will make it easier to rank and rate companies' impact on species conservation. Until then, check for the proxies discussed below.

Most of what you buy comes in some sort of packaging. Many plastics—including most polyethylene terephthalate (PET) plastic, clear films, waxlike coatings on food containers, and polystyrene— are not recyclable. Yet many companies are making good headway in decreasing overall packaging and increasing packaging made from recycled materials. For example, Unilever committed to halve its use of nonrecycled plastic by 2025.[92]

Good News for Forests

In the European Union, new regulations in 2024 require any company importing coffee, cocoa, soy, palm oil, wood, rubber, and cattle to prove that the products are not directly or indirectly causing deforestation. This may result in global companies, such as Danone, Nestlé, and Unilever, providing customers with the same deforestation-free products everywhere, not only in Europe.

What a company decides to make and innovate is like the rudder on a ship. It sets the course for the company's environmental impact. For example, a company can innovate products that support the environment by helping people reduce energy and water consumption in their daily activities, fostering biodiversity in food crops, and eliminating waste with closed-loop systems.

Laundry detergent is a good example. About 90 percent of the energy used to wash clothes comes from heating the water for a warm- or hot-water load.[93] Brands such as Tide, Gain, Persil, Seventh Generation, and Arm & Hammer innovated to offer detergents that are as effective in cold water as in hot water. This small change nudges millions of households to stop washing in hot water, saving energy and reducing carbon emissions.

Some companies strive to support the planet both by what they make and how they make it. Apparel brand Four Objects—my favorite source of chic, long-lasting clothes—embeds environmental responsibility into all aspects of the business. Four Objects uses only natural fibers because they are biodegradable. I could bury my favorite coat, and it would eventually become a part of the soil. The company adheres to a no-waste model and works with fabric suppliers that share the same values. They take back all their clothing, be it customer returns or end of life, and repair and resell or recycle them. Four Objects is a B Corp and created a business model that will continue to reflect its values as the company grows. It builds an annual collection of four pieces for its loyal customers and does not overproduce. Imagine if all fashion companies applied the same effort to reduce their impact.

New Materials and Regenerative Practices

New materials are changing fashion, home furnishings, and previously plastic items such as toys and garden furniture with the aim of reducing stress on the environment. Some next-gen materials are set to replace synthetic fabrics, such as polyester, with materials such as spider silk and viscose made from coconut water. Other materials transform waste such as biomass into new fabrics that feel like cotton, silk, or leather.

Move over, plastic leather—new materials are here. Most leather alternatives are made from plastics, polyurethane, or polyvinyl chloride, which are generally environmentally unfriendly. Today, new materials—including those made from old tires, plant protein, and mushrooms—are viable options. For example, apparel brands Tory Burch, Everlane, and Senreve sell fashion-statement handbags made of plant protein and old tires, a new technology produced by climate-tech innovators Modern Meadows. What a great way to keep old tires out of landfills, rivers, and incinerators! High-end designers make furniture, raincoats, and handbags from reishi mushroom material produced by MycoWorks and other companies. Keep an eye out for them!

Regenerative business practices go beyond sustainability. They take a systems approach and seek to restore and regenerate both communities and the planet. The goal is to go beyond reducing harm to actively restore and revitalize natural and social systems.

Sound lofty? Consider regenerative agriculture. It focuses on improving soil health, enhancing biodiversity, and restoring the neighboring environment. It does this by minimizing soil tilling, using cover crops and crop rotation, and planting perennials that maintain roots all year—which helps good soil microorganisms.

The pursuit of ways to produce goods that are regenerative drives innovation. For example, Parley for the Oceans (Parley), a nonprofit, partnered with Adidas to develop new shoe materials from marine plastic waste. Adidas integrates Primeblue, a high-performance yarn made from Parley's recycled ocean waste. It's one drop in the ocean of our waste problem, yet Adidas is advancing one step closer to regenerating the oceans.

YOUR SHOPPING SUPERPOWER TIPS AND TOOLS

After years of using a dining room chair in my home office, my back squawked. It was time to get a real office chair, one that supported my back and my values. I chose a chair from Herman Miller, a company with a wide-reaching and well-documented commitment to environmental sustainability. Its innovative use of ocean plastics, aggressive 2030 climate goals, and efforts to support biodiversity are impressive. The office chairs are made-to-order to reduce waste, and waiting for my chair added the joy of anticipation.

I considered many chairs in my selection process and settled on the lower-end chair as it offered all the same environmental benefits as pricier options. Many manufacturers offer a wide range of price points and produce them with equal care for the environment. You don't have to buy the most expensive item to live your environmental values.

You can shop across a range of prices for all types of products that are made with care for the environment. This includes one-off purchases such as an office chair, infrequent purchases such as jeans, as well as everyday grocery items. By doing so, you'll send signals that more environmentally friendly products are needed.

To make one impactful change a week, you can look for certifications, check rating systems, and avoid the worst offenders. And don't forget to tell brands you care! At the end of the chapter, you'll find a summary of the tools for easy decision-making.

Tip #1: Make One Impactful Change a Week

Like changing any habit, it's easier to make one small change per week than one big wholesale shift. Consider prioritizing switches for routinely purchased items that have positive ripple effects across many ecological systems. For example, your purchases from companies that support sustainable forests also help to protect biodiversity and address climate impacts. Similarly, products that minimize plastics and waste help to ease stress on waterways and reduce carbon emissions. Support regenerative agriculture, and you'll also support sustainable soil management, reduce climate impacts of food production, and enhance biodiversity in prairies and crops.

Routine Purchases to Switch for Impact

Here are the first products to switch because of their wide-ranging negative impacts. Start by changing out one of these in your weekly shopping:

Single-use plastics impact waste, water, soil, and climate. Swap away from disposable plastics, and you may save money over time. For much of this, you know the drill. Avoid single-use plastic bags, to-go cups, and plastic bottles. Disposable cutlery is not recyclable. Try bringing your own picnic set instead. Replace plastic produce bags with washable nets and plastic food wrap with beeswaxed food cloths. Try replacing disposable wet-wipe cleaning cloths with cotton dishtowels and old T-shirts for rags. Look for a shop that refills empty bottles with shower gel, laundry detergent bottles, and other products. Also consider cleaning materials in dry or pellet form. Consider investing in a durable razor and replace the blades as needed.

Palm oil is a major driver of large-scale deforestation. To avoid it, you'll need to look for products that state "No palm oil" or read labels carefully. WWF estimates that about 50 percent of all packaged products in the United States contain palm oil.

Choose one product a week to make switches to products without palm oil. Check baked goods and snacks you buy for palm oil, including bread, cakes, cookies, crackers, ice cream, and cake mixes. Also watch out for palm oil in cooking oil, shortening, and frying fats. It's also commonly found in breakfast bars, butter substitutes, and peanut butter, as well as in lipstick, soap, and detergent.

If products without palm oil are hard to find, choose ones with "sustainable palm oil."

Packaging waste is a bugbear. It's everywhere. To start, buy products in minimal viable packaging. Does fresh produce need to come in a plastic box? Look for the brands that dare to sell their products without unnecessary boxes. For example, toothpaste, deodorant, and most cosmetics don't need to come in a box.

And don't be fooled. Studies show that shoppers perceive a product's packaging as more environmentally friendly if a plastic bottle or tube is packaged in a cardboard box, even though a similar product from the same brand is available in just a plastic bottle.

For online shopping, look at the description of the products' packaging. Also look for biodegradable and compostable packing worms, paper fillers, and minimal glues or tape.

Note that there are no standards for what "minimal packaging" means. Tip #2 and Tip #3 provide you with a list of trustworthy certifications, databases, and directories to use to find products that meet your values in supporting the environment.

Occasional Purchases to Switch for Impact

Once you've become familiar with shopping with the environment in mind, you can start to integrate environmental considerations into your plans for items you buy occasionally. Start by focusing on the aspects of the environment you care most about.

Care about climate change? Buy durable items, because using natural resources and energy to make more replaceable stuff creates unnecessary carbon emissions. Avoid plastic things that will break after a few uses. Drop fast fashion. According to *Business Insider* and the United Nations Commission for Europe, fashion alone produces 8–10 percent of global carbon emissions. Instead, focus on buying long-lasting clothing made of natural fibers and washing in cold water. Avoid beef or buy local, grass-fed beef.

Energy and water efficiency your concern? When it's time to replace appliances, get hyperefficient ones for water and electricity use. The ratings discussed below provide good guidance. Consider buying jeans and other clothing items from companies committed to using less water. These products tend to require cold-only washing, which saves energy. Also look for cold-water detergents in dry form—a double saving for energy and packaging.

Hate the idea of deforestation? Commit first to buying paper and wood products only from certified sustainable sources. This includes toilet paper, office paper, furniture, and packaging materials. Look up all certifications on garden, home and office furniture, and guitars before buying to be sure they are genuinely sustainable. Be very careful of anything made from tropical hardwood.

Concerned about biodiversity loss and its risks to future food, medicine, and the wonders of the natural world? For fish, check the Marine Stewardship list (see below) to ensure that you're buying fish that are not threatened by overfishing. Encourage large grocery stores to require suppliers to prohibit the use of pesticides that are toxic to bees and other pollinators. Kroger, Walmart, and Whole Foods Market have all adopted this policy, which takes effect in 2025. Treat yourself to tasty heirloom fruits and vegetables. Support restaurants that do the same (see below). Avoid products linked to deforestation.

Want to support soil health and good land management? For food, look for regenerative meat products and organic foods, and buy from small-scale farmers. The regenerative movement is new and growing quickly; be an early adopter. Organic and small-scale farms are usually good stewards of the soil. For fashion, look for farm-to-textile options such as Nativa, used in fashion brands including Cos, Regeneration, and Vivienne Westwood.

Tip #2: Seek Trustworthy Certifications

Environmental certifications can help you identify products made to robust standards for specific aspects, such as energy use, organics, or sustainability. However, no environmental certification covers all aspects, and none is flawless. As discussed in Chapter 3, ardent environmentalists may consider some of the criteria and verification systems weak.

Below are the certifications I've researched and trust. They cover climate, biodiversity, land, water, and waste. Some of the certifications also cover aspects of labor and health, and thus may appear here and in other chapters.

You may find fake certification logos, created by companies to try to pass their products off as environmentally friendly. I've found a lot of misleading logos and marks on garden and home office furniture that make it appear that the furniture is made from sustainable wood. For example, one company's furniture came with a hangtag stating, "Responsible Forestry Practices" and featured a green leaf. At first glance, this looked good. However, the logo is not from a certified organization, and when I investigated it, I found that the company's website did not define "responsible forestry practices" nor indicate whether any third party verified their claims. The lack of transparency and details smacks of greenwash.

ENERGY STAR

ENERGY STAR certifies that products meet strict standards for energy efficiency. It covers home appliances, as well as products for commercial buildings and industrial plants. The ENERGY STAR program is run by the U.S. Environmental Protection Agency and the U.S. Department of Energy and is independently verified.

What products are certified and carry the seal? Almost anything that uses energy in your household, including most appliances, light bulbs, computers, televisions, and major household energy users, such water heaters and heating and cooling systems.

Where can you find this label? The ENERGY STAR website lists products and includes a search function for energy-efficiency rebates.

USDA Organic

USDA Organic produce supports soil health and protects waterways from pesticide runoff. The USDA Organic label is the only government -backed certification for organic food sold in the United States. The organic standard requires that operations use practices that recycle resources, conserve biodiversity, and preserve ecological balance.

What products are certified and carry the seal? Grains, produce, meat, eggs, dairy, and packaged products.

Where will you find this label? On products and brands in grocery stores and retailers, including big-box stores such as Walmart, Target, and Costco.

Rainforest Alliance (RA) Green Frog

Rainforest Alliance (RA) Green Frog supports farmers to produce better-quality, more sustainable, and more climate-resilient crops, which will enable the farmers to reduce costs, increase their productivity over time, and ultimately improve their livelihoods. I like this certification because it combines sustainable development, improved farmer incomes, and environmental concerns. It is only given to products with one or more key ingredients produced according to rigorous social, economic, and environmental sustainability standards.

What products are certified? Cocoa, coffee, flowers, plants, fruits, herbs, spices, nuts, tea, and vegetables.

Where will you find this label? Grocery stores, online, and Rainforest Alliance's product guide.

Green Seal

Green Seal, run by a U.S. nonprofit, covers a broad range of environmental and health concerns, including waste reduction, energy and water efficiency, reduced greenhouse gas emissions, and health safety. It applies external standards to validate its certification guidelines.

What products are certified? A range of categories, including cleaning products, paints, and construction materials.

Where will you find this label? Green Seal's product listing and Amazon's Climate Pledge Friendly listings.

Land to Market

Land to Market is a mark of regenerative agriculture and promotes soil health, biodiversity, carbon sequestration, and water cycle restoration. Land to Market uniquely ensures that the land is regenerating. It looks beyond agricultural inputs and asks if the soil is becoming healthier. Farmers and ranchers apply its science-based verification system to measure regenerative outcomes on their land. If you believe in the importance of regenerating land, this label is worth hunting for.

What products are certified and carry the seal? Hundreds of products, including meat, dairy, wool, wine, and leather, are certified and carry the seal.

Where will you find this label? On products and brands in grocery stores and retailers, including online. The Land to Market website features a product listing.

Ecocert

Ecocert is an independent inspection and certification company specializing in organic agriculture products. It has two key roles. In Europe, its mark is used on certified organic products that meet Ecocert's organic standards. Ecocert also undertakes certification processes for many certifiers, including USDA Organic for products grown outside the United States, GOTS (Global Organic Textile

Standard), OCS (Organic Content Standard), and COSMOS (Organic and Natural Standard). When serving as a certifier for others, Ecocert applies its organic standards.

What gets certified? Food products, cosmetics, raw materials, detergents, and textiles.

Where will I find this label? Ecocert is one of the largest certifiers of organic produce in the United States, certifying on behalf of USDA Organic. However, you will mostly see the USDA logo on U.S.-sold goods. In Europe, you'll find Ecocert labels on a wide range of products.

® Forest Stewardship Council (FSC)®

Forest Stewardship Council (FSC)–certified products are made from sustainably managed forests along the supply chain. FSC certification means zero deforestation over time. Old-growth and rare forests are identified and protected. The label also ensures that fair wages are paid to workers and that local communities are consulted. It's run by a not-for-profit organization, governed by a global network of more than 1,000 individuals and member organizations to ensure that broad and deep environmental, social, and economic perspectives are represented. It's the gold standard for wood products because all principles and criteria used in FSC certification are mandatory. There is no wiggle room to receive certification. The FSC has three different labels:

- FSC 100° percent. Entirely from FSC-certified, well-managed forests.
- FSC Recycled®. Everything comes from recycled material.

- FSC Mix®. Allows manufacturers to mix FSC-certified material with noncertified materials in FSC-labeled products under controlled conditions.

What products are certified and carry the seal? Anything with paper or pulp in it: paper, cardboard, packaging, tissue, paper cups, and timber, as well as cellulosic fibers used in fashion, shoes, and sports equipment, including rayon, viscose, lyocell, and modal.

Where will you find this label? On products sold everywhere.

Sustainable Forestry Initiative (SFI)

Sustainable Forestry Initiative (SFI) certifies wood products from North American forests and is the single largest forest certification standard in the world in terms of total certified area. It is an independent nonprofit organization, governed by an eighteen-member board of directors structured to purposefully ensure equal voting power to environmental, social, and economic sectors. SFI requirements for forest management, fiber sourcing, and chain-of-custody certification are independently audited by independent certification bodies.

What products are certified and carry the seal? Any wood or paper products containing fiber from North American forests certified to the SFI Standards.

Where will you find this label? On products sold everywhere, including product listings on SFI's website.

Marine Stewardship Council (MSC)

Marine Stewardship Council (MSC)'s standard requires fisheries to be assessed by an independent, third-party auditor to confirm that the seafood being caught comes from a healthy population that can reproduce for generations to come. The MSC requires tracking and accountability through the entire supply chain to help protect against seafood fraud.

What products are certified? More than 1,400 certified fish products—including fresh, frozen, packaged, and canned fish—are certified in the United States and Canada. Some pet foods and supplements are also certified.

Where will you find this label? The MSC website includes a database of retailers that stock MSC-certified fish.

Slow Food Snail of Approval

The Slow Food Snail of Approval is an award of excellence rather than a certification. It is awarded to food and beverage businesses committed to protecting biodiversity; supporting local communities, employees, and purveyors; and standing against racism and oppression. The award is unique in that it is given by local Slow Food chapters, not by a centralized national committee.

What gets certified? Restaurants, food and beverage producers.

Where will you find this label? Across the United States, Australia, New Zealand, and Barbados. Find your closest chapter online to discover local Snail of Approval products.

Cradle to Cradle Certified (C2C)

Cradle to Cradle Certified (C2C) products have circularity built into the design. Circularity means the company keeps resources in continual use by designing products so that customers return used parts or containers to be used again. (See Chapter 9 to learn about circular business models.) A product earns an achievement level—basic, bronze, silver, gold, or platinum—based on how it uses materials, water, and renewable energy, what it does for carbon management, and whether workers and others are treated fairly.

What gets certified? Apparel, home goods, toys, furniture, cleaning supplies, building materials, and more. Materials used in textiles, such as yarn, fabric, and dyes, can also be certified.

Where will you find this label? C2C runs a product registry, and you will see the certification on products in many online and physical retailers.

A Greener World

A Greener World certifies sustainable food grown and raised by independent farmers in North America in four categories: animal welfare, grass-fed, non-GMO, and regenerative. The standards were developed with scientists, veterinarians, experts, and farmers from around the world.

What gets certified? Products from independent farms, including meat, eggs, dairy, produce and grains, fiber and leather, crops, feed, seed and processed products.

Where will you find this label? Certified products are available throughout North America at local farmers' markets, co-ops, restaurants, online, through distributors, and in regional and national retail outlets. A Greener World runs a product registry. It's easiest to type in your location to see what products are available in your region.

Regenerative Organic Certified® (ROC™)

Regenerative Organic Certified (ROC) is a groundbreaking umbrella certification that represents the world's highest standard for organic agriculture, with stringent requirements for soil health and land management, pasture-based animal welfare, and farmworker fairness. ROC is a global standard covering millions of acres and engaging hundreds of brands globally.

What gets certified? Farms, food, beauty products, apparel, and other goods.

Where will you find this label? On thousands of products in the United States, most of which are listed on the ROC brand and product directory.

Climate Beneficial

Developed by the nonprofit Fibershed, Climate Beneficial–certified wool and cotton comes from farming systems that sequester more carbon than they emit. This exciting certification will expand to other materials as more farmers turn to regenerative practices.

What gets certified? Wool and cotton from farmers and producers in California.

Where will you find this label? Fibershed publishes a product list of its niche products. And I can't wait to see these offerings expand.

B Corporations (B Corps)

B Corps are for-profit companies that are driven by both mission and profit. B Corps must meet high standards of social and environmental performance, accountability, and transparency, and are legally required to consider the impact of their decisions on all stakeholders. In contrast, a standard company, a C Corporation (C Corp), is primarily focused on maximizing shareholder value and not required to meet any specific social or environmental standards beyond those mandated by law. The B Corp certification is verified by B Labs, a global nonprofit. It's a safe bet that any product from a B Corp is made with concern for the environment.

What companies are certified B Corp? B Corp companies come in all sizes, from multinationals to one-person start-ups. About 4,000 companies are registered as a B Corp. A few of the most well-known are Patagonia, Ben & Jerry's, Tom's, Warby Parker, Allbirds, Bombas, and Athleta.

Where will you find this label? You'll see the B Corp logo on the home page of company websites and on some products.

Tip #3: Rating Systems, Directories, and Apps

Apps and blogs that rate and compare products' environment impacts have evolved quickly. When you find one that might work for you, remember to check the following:

- Who runs it? Is it a for-profit retailer or company trying to sell you a product?
- What are the standards and ranking criteria? Can you easily find them?
- Are the assessments verified by a third party or scientific committee?

Avoid any ranking or rating system that does not clearly state how products are assessed. The sources below are transparent rankings and ratings for a variety of environmental issues.

Table 5.1. Databases and Directories on Environmental Impact

Database or Directory	Products Covered	What It Offers
Ark of Taste	Food biodiversity	An international crowdsourced database of foods that people see disappearing from their communities
Chocolate Score Card	Chocolate	Ranks chocolate brands, including retailers with house brands, on deforestation and climate, agroforestry, and pesticide use, along with three social measures
Cluey Consumer	All products	This smart app rates brands based on their impact on people, the planet, and politics, with A to F ratings. The app is transparent about its algorithm, vetting process, and business model.

Table 5.1. Databases and Directories on Environmental Impact (Continued)

Database or Directory	Products Covered	What It Offers
Conscious Customer	Eco-products, household chemicals, food	Search for options that are less harmful to the environment and your health. Funded by the EU and verified by experts. Not as deep as Environmental Working Group (EWG), but covers more foods.
Good On You	Fashion	A rating system that captures many aspects of a fashion brand's impact on people and the planet. The system includes climate and waste management, types of fibers, sustainability of business model, product durability, and commitment to reuse of inputs. The scale runs from "we avoid" to "great."
NatureHub	General shopping	Searchable by what values matter to you (nature, workers, organic). NatureHub connects you with participating local businesses, products, and other resources. Covers environmental and social issues. Great for larger cities.
Palm Oil Scan	Foods, drinks, pet products, and household and personal care items	A group of zoos created this app to help you find products made from sustainable palm oil to protect forests and specifically orangutans, whose habitat is under threat from palm oil plantations. You can either search for a product or scan a barcode.
Palm Oil Score Card	Major retailers and brands of food, household and personal care items, and home furnishings	Ranks brands and retailers on five topics: commitments to purchase palm oil that is free from deforestation, land conversion, and human rights violations; how much palm oil purchased is covered by RSPO certification; suppliers requirements; member of one or more action-oriented sustainable palm oil platforms; and on-the-ground investments
PFAS Central	All products	List of PFAS-free products

Table 5.1. Databases and Directories on Environmental Impact (Continued)

Database or Directory	Products Covered	What It Offers
Remake	Fashion	Annual comprehensive evaluation and ranking of top 50 fashion companies, including environmental standards
Too Good to Go	Food waste	This app matches you with local stores and restaurants selling surprise bags of surplus food. A great way to stop food waste. Many companies donate your payment to charity.

Many shopping platforms specialize in environmentally friendly products. The largest is Amazon's Climate Pledge Friendly products. To be listed, products must be certified by one or more of the twenty-three different sustainability certifications, including most listed under Tip #2. Remember to always check the criteria for eco-friendly commerce platforms and how they are verified.

Tip #4: Avoid the Worst Offenders

Most environmental damage and release of greenhouse gases come from fossil fuels that are integrated into our economy and daily life. While economy-wide changes are necessary to address these forces directly, you can easily avoid the worst offenders by doing the following:

- Avoid products that are energy inefficient, including cars and home appliances.
- Change your home energy provider to a green, renewable source.

- Reject products that are unnecessarily disposable: plastic bags, coffee pods, plastic forks and knives, single-use razors, drinks in single-use plastic bottles, and so on.
- Avoid all nonbiodegradable plastics—including in electronics, toys, straws, containers, bags, and more—because they will never fully break down and will release toxins into the environment.
- Avoid using products with phosphates, which create algae blooms in water and use up the oxygen available to sustain marine life.

How to Find Sustainable Fish and Seafood

These two seafood guides help you avoid endangered fish and seafood:

- The Marine Stewardship Council (MSC) manages a database on its website of brands, retailers, and chain restaurants that carry MSC-certified fish products.
- The Monterey Bay Aquarium's Seafood Watch consumer guides to which fish to eat is searchable by fish species or your location by region. The regional guides and sushi guide can be downloaded or printed, folded, and carried in your wallet.

Tip #5: Tell the Brand You Care

You may be frustrated by a favorite brand's lack of good environmentally friendly options. Tell them! This is one of the easiest and most impactful things you can do. Brands are sensitive to their customers' thoughts and feelings because brand reputation is everything.

To start your note, let the brand know that you are already a loyal customer, a first-time buyer, or considering switching to their brand.

Here are four basic templates you can then use as a starting point. These templates are only provided as a guide. Get creative and use your own words.

1. "I am a loyal customer and love [*product name*]. I care deeply about the environment and want to be certain that my purchases support a better world. Can you please tell me about your company's sustainability goals? I don't see them on your company website. Will you publish them with regular reports on progress for all to see? If I don't see a report in the next twelve months, I will consider switching to a brand that states goals and reports."

2. "I purchased [*this product*] from [*this grocery store, this online retailer*]. Though I like [*the taste, the product*], I am disappointed that it's packaged in [*single-use plastic, unnecessary cardboard, unrecycled material*]. Those materials are [*challenging to recycle, unable to be composted in home compost, unable to be recycled or reused*]. Have you considered packaging that is more easily recycled or repurposed? This matters to me! I will consider switching to an eco-friendlier brand if your brand does not reduce waste."

3. "I am a fan of [*this product*]. Still, I am disappointed that you use unsustainable [*palm oil, imported beef*] in [*this product*]. As these ingredients/materials are known to [*harm the environment, lead to deforestation*], I will not purchase this product again unless your formula changes."

4. "I support regenerative and organic farming. I like [*your product*] but want more sustainable options. Can you increase the percentage of [*produce, meat, dairy, and packaged goods*] that come from certified regenerative agriculture or organic sources?"

SUMMING IT UP

Focus on one change a week. It may seem overwhelming at first but keep going with one small change a week. Here's where to start:

Table 5.2. High-Impact Switches for Frequent and Infrequent Purchases

Frequent Purchases	Special Occasion or Infrequent Purchases
Climate and Waste	
Stop buying single-use plastics. Swap disposable products for durable ones, including cutlery, shopping and produce bags, wet wipes, food wrap, razors. Swap liquid for powder or dry options, including shampoo, laundry detergent and softener, toothpaste, hand soap. Switch to cold-wash-only detergents.	Fashion: Buy long-lasting clothes made from natural fibers from companies committed to sustainable fashion.
	Appliances, cars, tools: Buy the most energy- and water-efficient appliances within your budget, including smart faucets and water filters, low-flow showerheads, and dual-flush toilets.
	Read company websites and switch to products made by companies that have strong greenhouse gas emissions reduction goals and/or 100 percent renewable energy goals.
Deforestation, Biodiversity, Water, and Land Management	
Switch everyday products with palm oil for brands that don't contain it, including baked goods, snacks, cooking oils, beverages, breakfast bars, margarine, nut butters, lipstick, soap, and detergent.	Furniture, guitars, and other items made from wood: Buy only FSC-certified or recycled timber.

Table 5.2. High-Impact Switches for Frequent and Infrequent Purchases (Continued)

Frequent Purchases	Special Occasion or Infrequent Purchases
Deforestation, Biodiversity, Water, and Land Management	
Buy chocolate that ranks well on the Chocolate Score Card or is certified by Rainforest Alliance or a similar organization.	Buy household furnishings, sports, outdoor gear, and other clothes that are PFAS-free and sourced from certified sustainable wood.
Switch to U.S.-grass-fed or -certified regenerative beef.	Buy clothes or accessories made from next-generation materials that replace leather and plastics.
Don't buy fish on the MSC watch list.	Buy products made from recycled ocean plastic waste, such as tennis shoes and garden furniture.
Look for heritage varieties of fruits, vegetables, and grains. Try something new!	Choose a Snail of Approval restaurant for a special occasion.
Double-check materials used in packaging for online goods. Donate online purchases rather than return goods that don't match your expectations.	Prioritize compostable packaging and compost it with your veggie scraps.

As you start to unleash your shopping superpower, you'll help shape the economy in ways that align with your values. Remember, consumer demand drives about 70 percent of the U.S. economy. Use your spending power to help protect and restore the environment by making one switch a week.

Chapter 6

COMMUNITY: BUY LOCAL AND FROM BUSINESSES WITH DIVERSE OWNERSHIP

Miriam, an undergraduate at a local college, sells me a plump chicken. She's the face of her family's butcher business at my local farmers' market. She always asks how I will cook it. A few steps away, the coffee roaster remembers I buy decaf beans. I don't recall his name, but I know he loves to fish. Bread? Douglas sells loaves made from organic midwestern grains. I salivate thinking about his bread, toasted for breakfast.

During the pandemic, farmers' markets became my lifeline. Every Saturday morning, I met and chatted with the folks who grew and made most of what I'd eat the following week. Weekly visits to the farmers' market continue to bring me joy.

Buying locally is more than a way of keeping me grounded and stocked with fresh produce. It's vital for the economic health of my community.

Similarly, buying from businesses owned by women and minorities is a tangible way to affect underlying economic inequalities based on gender, race, and systemic poverty. Minority- and women-owned businesses have a much tougher time getting bank loans than businesses owned by white males.[94, 95] That's why steady, reliable business is critical for their cash flow and growth.

The biggest challenge to shopping locally is the convenience of shopping online. Amazon and other online retailers tempt shoppers with a crazy array of choices, product reviews, and next-day delivery. It's addictive. Yet something is missing with online shopping—the curation of products by a local shop, the gentle chitchat and pleasantries, and feeling like a regular, valued patron. Furthermore, what type of community do you want? Do you want one that has thriving local businesses? If you don't support local businesses, are you okay with your town becoming a stretch of big-box stores with Amazon lockers?

Small and local businesses have it tough. With added pressure from the pandemic and inflation, it's no wonder that local shops are closing at a rate higher than pre-pandemic. One out of five small businesses in the United States fail in the first year, and only about half survive five years or more.[96]

The trend of local shops closing will change only when you and I are very intentional about where we shop. It's not easy. Habits—and the addiction to online convenience—are hard to overcome. Start small. Make one change a week to purchase something locally or from a women- or minority-owned business. It can be a coffee at a locally owned coffee shop, vegetables at a farmers' market, or a gift or seasonal piece of clothing from a local boutique. Switch something once a week.

The impact of your shopping adds up quickly—and it may make you feel more connected and happier.

In the first part of this chapter, you'll learn:

- about the vital role of local, independent businesses
- how much positive impact you can easily have on a small local business
- the value of supporting businesses owned by women, minorities, and uncelebrated proprietors

In the second section, you'll find tips on where to start making changes and tools to help you find these types of businesses and shops.

Note that retailers often sell things made by another company. The ownership of both the retailer and the producer matters. You can look for both—local and minority-owned retailers and service providers, and local and minority-owned producers. For example, I often look online for beauty products made by minority-owned companies and at my grocery store for locally made salsas and condiments.

VITAL FOR THE ECONOMIC HEALTH OF YOUR COMMUNITY

If you want a vibrant community, shop locally.

Every time you buy something at an independent local shop, it creates a virtuous cycle of growth. Think of it as a continuous positive-feedback loop. Your purchase helps the shop grow, which creates jobs and feeds the local economy with taxes and direct spending. The employees of the shop spend more locally, and the circle grows.

Why Buy Local

Local businesses circulate 4x the money in the local economy compared to chain stores.

Local businesses create jobs for their local community.

Local businesses support local events, sport teams & charities 250% more than big corporations.

Local businesses stock local products catering to their community's needs and tastes.

Three times more money stays in the local economy when you shop locally. In a local shop, about forty-eight cents out of every dollar of revenue recirculate in your community.[97] Wages, benefits, and profits stay local. This compares with less than fourteen cents per dollar from a chain store.[98] If you shop online, only about 8 cents per dollar of revenue remains in your community.[99]

In addition, locally owned businesses tend to create more jobs in your community than chain stores. In some sectors, locally owned businesses provide better wages and benefits. When a business spends locally to buy office supplies or hires local accounting, marketing, and cleaning services, it builds a virtuous cycle, and your local economy expands as dollars circulate within the community.

Eating out? Independent restaurants reinvest more than twice as much money per dollar of sales into their own communities, compared with national restaurant chains.[100]

Most grocery stores are owned by large corporations.[101] As a result, the profits from your local store go to the corporation rather than staying in the local community. My friend Cynthia does almost all her shopping at a corner mom-and-pop shop. Why? Because she knows that her spending helps feed the shop owners' families and pay their rent. Plus, the smiles and regular exchange of pleasantries are a welcome bonus. In many communities, small grocery stores have disappeared. Your options? Some national chains sell local produce (see Tip #1 below), and your area may have a good farmers' market (see Tip #3 below).

How Much Impact Do I Really Have?

For a coffee shop to turn a small profit, it takes twenty paying patrons an hour during peak hours.[102] By regularly dropping in each morning for a coffee, you can make a big enough difference to help your local shop thrive. You can become 5 percent of your coffee shop's hourly business. Bring your own reusable cup and help reduce waste.

When you eat twice a month with a group of four people at a local restaurant, you help create a stable financial base for the business.[103]

Similarly, a farmers' market needs about one hundred people a day[104] to be viable, depending on location costs. When you go with a few friends or family members, you make a sizable impact on what's required.

Keep an eye out for how much local companies give back to your community. Local shops tend to support school sports, the arts, and other municipal activities through either cash or in-kind donations. Even small gestures help build community. Do your local coffee shop or other businesses provide refreshments for arts or sports events?

Locally owned businesses can source from nearby communities, further benefiting local farmers and craftspeople. For example, a young woman in a nearby town started sewing children's clothes, and our local clothing shop now stocks them.

Local shops can curate their offerings to match your needs and tastes. National chains and franchises create centralized sales plans, so you'll find only what someone in a distant city decided you would want. Someone in New York City may not know when it's mud season in Boulder or how cold a New Mexican winter is.

Another bonus of shopping locally: It generally reduces packaging and waste. No excess packaging or cardboard boxes from online delivery. Bring your own cloth tote bag, and you'll have no packaging waste.

Confessions of Compromise

Amazon displaced tens of thousands of local shops pre-pandemic.[105] "Displaced" is a sanitized term for killing these businesses. But it's just so easy to shop online, I am often torn between convenience and my values. I'm not alone in this feeling.

In the United States, more than six out of ten consumers look first on Amazon when they want to buy something, and almost half of all online spending goes to Amazon.[106] Yet the pandemic shifted how we think about online shopping and small businesses. More people became aware of the value of local and minority-owned businesses. Search interest for "ethical online shopping" grew 600 percent year over year in 2020.[107] In the same period, searches seeking out "Black-owned shops" grew ninefold.[108]

Everyone needs to find their own balance. Being aware is the first step.

BUSINESSES OWNED BY WOMEN, BLACK, INDIGENOUS PEOPLE, AND OTHER PEOPLE OF COLOR

By itself, shopping can't erase sexism or racism. However, you can start to chip away at systemic inequalities by thoughtfully wielding your wallet.

Women business owners don't have it easy. When it comes to getting financial support to grow, they face discrimination. About 40 percent of U.S. businesses are women owned, yet banks grant only about 16 percent of all business loans to women.[109] What's more, these loans are smaller than those to male-owned businesses—by a shocking amount. Women-owned small businesses in 2022 received loans that were nearly 40 percent less, on average, than businesses owned by men.[110]

Most women fund their business ventures by bootstrapping with cash flow, personal savings, and personal credit rather than business loans. Without start-up capital or an infusion of cash, they can't invest more in their businesses. No wonder women-owned businesses tend to start and stay smaller, bringing in less revenue than male-owned businesses.[111]

Shopping at women-owned businesses gives you a direct way to fight this inequality. When you support women-owned businesses, you're saying that you disagree with discriminatory banking practices and want to see business owned by women thrive. You're also letting women know that you value their contribution to the community, appreciate their products, and want the choice and customer service that their businesses offer.

The situation is worse for minority-owned businesses. One out of five small businesses in the United States is minority owned. Yet these owners receive less financing from banks and the government than other groups, and they pay higher interest rates than white business owners.[112] This discrepancy included the U.S. Paycheck Protection Program (PPP) loans during the pandemic. Small minority-owned businesses received less than 2 percent of all PPP loans.[113]

It's also more of a hassle for many minority business owners to access financing. Minority business owners are more often asked to show business financial statements, income tax returns, and other documents, including personal financial details, compared to white business owners.[114]

UNCELEBRATED PROPRIETORS

Businesses owned and run by veterans, refugees, and people with disabilities strengthen and diversify local economies. These entrepreneurs bring unique perspectives, skills, and experiences to communities, often drawing on their military service, cross-cultural knowledge, or adaptive problem-solving abilities. Their ventures create jobs and often bring innovation to the community, yet they often face unique hurdles. For example, veterans may struggle with transitioning their military skills to civilian entrepreneurship. Refugees often encounter language barriers and unfamiliarity with local habits. People with disabilities may need to navigate physical accessibility issues or overcome societal misconceptions about their capabilities. Despite these hurdles, many of these business owners demonstrate remarkable resilience and creativity and build successful enterprises.

Veterans

Supporting a veteran-owned business is a direct way to thank them for their military service. Veterans who served our country are 45 percent more likely to be self-employed than nonveterans.[115] I find this fact astonishing. It makes me want to support these service-minded do-it-yourselfers.

Military spouses—wives and husbands—often face barriers to traditional employment because of frequent relocations. Running their own service businesses, such as accounting, translation, and editing, is a solution for many military spouses. For example, R. Riverter makes hand-stitched leather and canvas handbags, candles, and other items by decentralized production, which enables military spouses to work remotely. Each piece is stamped by the person who made it.

Refugees

Refugees arrive under extreme circumstances, having been forced to flee their country because of persecution, war, or violence.[116] Generally, they're highly motivated to build a new life and create some stability for their families. More than 180,000 refugees run businesses in the United States,[117] bringing new skills, foods, art, and culture to our communities. Unfortunately, there is no centralized national list or certification program for refugee-owned businesses. You need to look around and ask your Chamber of Commerce or local church groups.

You also can support businesses that commit to hiring refugees. For example, women-owned Open Arms Studio is a made-in-the-United States, cut-and-sew production studio for apparel and soft furnishings. It's an alternative to outsourcing manufacturing to overseas sweatshops. Based in Austin, Texas, the company is committed to training and hiring refugees and paying fair wages. Similarly, women-owned Prosperity Candles, a great go-to for gifts, hires refugees and offers them good work, community, and a path forward.

People with Disabilities

People with disabilities often must overcome discrimination, physical challenges, and other barriers to run their businesses. Despite the hurdles, roughly 15 percent of people with disabilities have started their own businesses. This is a higher percentage than people without disabilities.[118]

LGBTQ+ Businesses

LGBTQ+ businesses contribute about $1.7 trillion to the U.S. economy each year.[119] With no federal certification available, the National Gay and Lesbian Chamber of Commerce created a certification program to give business owners from within the LGBTQ+ community a boost and undertake research to understand if and how these business owners might face discrimination.

SUPPORTING COMPANIES THAT SUPPORT EQUAL EMPLOYMENT OPPORTUNITIES

Starting a business is not for everyone, and a good job can be magic for the right person. Companies are legally required to treat everyone fairly, including women, minorities, veterans, refugees, people with disabilities, and people who served time in prison. Despite these regulations, discrimination persists. This is why I pay attention to companies that support equal employment opportunities in meaningful ways, above and beyond what the law requires.

Businesses are starting to recognize the talents and gifts that neurodiverse employees bring to their jobs. In the hotel sector, Virgin leads the way. A hotel group with an impressive environmental program employs neurodiverse teammates. It trains all its staff so that neurodiverse employees have the best working environment for their needs. "They bring value and special skills that others don't have," explains David Moth, vice president of operations at Virgin Hotels. Other hotel companies, such as Marriott, are following Virgin's leadership and expanding hiring programs.

Deciding Between Two Good Choices

Many companies actively engaged in neurodiverse hiring are big tech companies, banks, and hotel chains. Most people will not switch software providers over this issue. But what about banking? Do you support a local bank that sticks to minimum efforts required by law but supports local community events? Or do you switch to a global bank that has a well-established program for neurodiverse employees?

Take such a decision in two steps. First, decide which positive impact you value more: community banking or supporting neurodiverse people? Remember your superpower principles. There are no right or wrong answers. Make your call based on what you value most. Second, find ways to double your support of the type of business you didn't first select. If you stay with your community bank, look for other businesses that support neurodiverse employees.

You may find local businesses that seek to hire people with disabilities. For example, Frida Pickles is a flower and gift shop in Los Angeles founded to provide good employment opportunities for neurodiverse people and those with special needs. They pay above minimum wage for all employees and adapt to each employee's specific needs. "When a customer shops here, their purchase helps us expand towards our mission of creating other businesses for more diverse job opportunities," explains Frida Pickles' co-owner Susan Sanchez. The flower shop survived the pandemic, thanks to regular customers.

Currently there isn't a single directory to find the shops and businesses that embrace the skills and talents of neurodiverse people. In the meantime, such businesses are best found by word of mouth, media coverage, or dedicated Internet searches.

Previously Incarcerated Employees

I became interested in the employment dilemmas facing people with a criminal record while working for Sir Richard Branson at his Virgin Group. Branson strongly believes in second chances. He also thinks that hiring those who were incarcerated increases the talent pool, lowers the price tag of reoffending, nurtures the entrepreneurial spirit, and contributes to safer communities.

This is no small issue. According to the Federal Bureau of Investigation (FBI), almost one out of every three people in the United States has a criminal background. The FBI considers anyone who has been arrested on a felony charge to have a criminal record, even if he or she is not convicted, and counts a misdemeanor if a state agency asks the bureau to keep it on file.[120] A criminal record reduces the likelihood of a second interview or job offer by a whopping 50 percent, hindering the abilities of people with criminal backgrounds to succeed.[121]

The Taste of Social Justice

If you've ever had Ben & Jerry's Chocolate Fudge Brownie or Half-Baked ice cream flavors, you've had a taste of social justice. The brownie in the ice cream is made by Grayston Bakery, a company that creates jobs for people who otherwise might remain jobless.

Grayston Bakery has a groundbreaking open-door hiring policy: Anyone who wants a job is given a chance to work. Their educational background doesn't matter, nor does their work history, nor past social barriers such as incarceration, homelessness, or drug use.[122] There are no background checks. There's no prescreening. It's simple: When a position becomes available, the next person on the waiting list gets it, no questions asked.

Don't be fooled into thinking that this is some recent small start-up funded by a tech-world dropout. Grayston has been baking brownies since 1982 and started supplying Ben & Jerry's in 1988. It currently sells brownies to airlines, grocery stores, and online.

Go get a pint and two spoons to share the joy.

YOUR SHOPPING SUPERPOWER TIPS AND TOOLS

Last summer I noticed a tiny sign for coffee, pointing down a side street in a nearby town. After a few steps, I smelled roasting coffee. After a few more steps, I found a veteran-owned coffee roaster. And it's delicious coffee!

How do you find these gems on your own? You don't have to follow your nose or rely on luck. In this section, you'll discover ideas about where to start, plus tools and tips to locate businesses owned and operated by people in your community—women, minorities, veterans, refugees, and people with disabilities. You'll find easy and time-efficient tips to meaningfully support these businesses and a summary to simplify decision-making.

Tip #1: Make One Impactful Change a Week

Start with small changes that are easy and make an impact. Groceries, coffee, meals out, and gifts are good places to start. One of the most routine things purchased is groceries. It may seem counterintuitive to check your grocery store for local produce, yet many national grocery stores are good sources of local produce and locally made goods. Local produce is often fresher than produce that has been trucked or flown from afar. Fruits and vegetables can be riper, more flavorful, and even more nutritious than those that travel long distances. Local products with a long shelf life—such as salsas, jams, pickles, sauces, sweets, coffee, and tea—might be less expensive because transportation costs are lower.

Here are some grocery store chains known for carrying local produce:

Whole Foods Market (national)
Heinen's (Illinois and Ohio)
Sprouts (West Coast)
Hy-ve (Midwest)
Wegmans (East Coast)
H.E.B. (Texas and New Mexico)
Publix (South)
Hannaford (Northeast)
Central Market (Texas)

For impact beyond groceries, look for opportunities to buy from uncelebrated proprietors, overlooked community members, or minority-owned businesses. "Don't just buy any gift. Buy a gift that matters to humans," says Susan Sanchez, co-owner of Frida Pickles. For example, try buying a gift from one of the platforms listed under Tip #3. Consider which group of business owners you want to support the most—women, minorities, LGBTQ+, people with disabilities, veterans who have served our country, or another group—and start there. The charts at the end of this chapter offer another way forward when choosing products. There you'll find suggested swap-outs for routine purchases such as coffee, baby supplies, bakery items, and restaurants, as well as occasional purchases such as jewelry, plants, and craft supplies.

Tip #2: Seek Trustworthy Certifications

Third-party certifications are a quick way to verify that a business is at least 51 percent owned, operated, and controlled by women, minorities, veterans, persons with disabilities, or members of the LGBTQ+ community. Applicants go through an exacting process to earn the certification. You'll see these trustworthy certification logos on shop windows or on website home pages. Keep an eye out for them.

Women's Business Enterprise, Women-Owned Business, and Women-Owned Small Business

Women Business Enterprise (WBE) and Women Owned Business (WOB) certifications are the most widely recognized and respected national certification for women-owned businesses in the United States. These certifications are administered by the Women's Business Enterprise National Council (WBENC). For small businesses, look for the Women Owned Small Business (WOSB) certification, administered by the U.S. Small Business Administration (SBA).

What businesses are certified? Companies that are at least 51 percent unconditionally and directly owned and controlled by one or more women who are U.S. citizens. A certified WOSB company must be small in its industry, as determined by the SBA.

Where will you find this label? Look on storefronts, websites, and online lists and directories, including Amazon's women-owned business storefront.

Gender Fair

Gender Fair rates companies on the extent to which they support gender equity. The rating metrics are based on the United Nations' Women's Empowerment Principles, which look at how a company treats women inside the company and in the communities it serves. The resulting rating is binary: Gender Fair or Not. A 100-point scoring system backs up this simple rating.

What products are certified? The award rating is given at the company level, and you will not find the certification logo on individual products.

Where will you find this label? Look on company websites. Gender Fair's app and Chrome extension will let you instantly check for fairness. The rankings cover more than 20,000 organizations, including companies, universities, and nonprofit organizations.

Minority Business Enterprise (MBE)

Minority Business Enterprise (MBE) certification is the most widely recognized and respected national certification for minority-owned businesses in the United States.

What businesses are certified? This certification requires 51 percent or more ownership by members of the following racial or ethnic minorities:

- African American/Black
- Asian-Indian American
- Asian-Pacific American/Asian-Islander American
- Native American Indian
- Hispanic

Where will you find this label? Look on storefronts, websites, and online lists and directories. Amazon and other retail platforms have minority-owned storefronts.

Note that many Native American tribes certify businesses run by their tribal members. However, there's no centralized list of these certified businesses. The MBE certification covers all tribal member–owned businesses. See below for a directory of products.

ByBlack

The ByBlack Platform is a certification and online business directory powered by the U.S. Black Chambers, Inc.

What businesses are certified? The business must be at least 51 percent Black-owned, managed, operated and be headquartered in the United States, and be in operation for at least one year.

Where will you find this label? The online directory is a rich source for finding local and national businesses, including a cities-based listing. Check your local African American Chamber of Commerce for events.

Native American Made Products

The Native American Made Products certification signals that the products are made by Native Americans from federally recognized tribes and Alaskan Native villages in the United States. Misrepresentation of Native American–made products is illegal and unethical. The Intertribal Agriculture Council (IAC) created and promotes the Made/Produced by American Indians trademark to clearly identify American Indian–made products.

What products are certified? Food products, jewelry, gifts, apparel, and more.

Where will you find this label? The IAC's booklet, available on its website, is a good resource to find qualified producers. Some products, such as food products, will include the logo on the label. Others are listed on the American Indian Foods website.

Veteran Owned Businesses

Veteran Owned Businesses certifications include four different categories:

• Veteran Owned Business (VOB) certification is the broadest category and covers all businesses owned 51 percent or more by a veteran.

- Service Disabled Veteran Owned Small Business certification recognizes veterans disabled through their military service.
- Veteran Disability Owned Business Enterprises recognizes those whose disability was not incurred during their time of service.
- Veteran Owned Small Businesses is run by the U.S. Small Business Administration (SBA).

What businesses are certified? This certification requires 51 percent or more ownership by veterans. Qualification of small businesses are determined by the SBA.

Where will you find this label? Look on storefronts, websites, and online lists and directories. Amazon has a veterans' business storefront.

Disability Owned Business Enterprise (DOBE)

The Disability Owned Business Enterprise (DOBE) certification signals that you're buying from a business owned by a person with a disability.

What businesses are certified? This certification signals that the business is at least 51 percent owned, operated, controlled, and managed by a person with a disability.

Where will you find this label? Look on storefronts, websites, and online lists and directories.

National LGBT Chamber of Commerce (NGLCC)

The National LGBT Chamber of Commerce (NGLCC) designation is available to businesses that are at least 51 percent owned, operated, managed, and controlled by an LGBTQ+ person or persons who are legal residents in the United States. There is currently no logo, and fewer than 2,000 enterprises are registered with the LGBT Chamber of Commerce.

What businesses are certified? All businesses that qualify under the National LGBT Chamber of Commerce standards.

Where will you find certified businesses? Check the NGLCC Business Directory for retail stores, professional services, hospitality, health and wellness, creative industries, and the technology sector.

Tip #3: Rating Systems, Directories, and Apps

Specialized directories and apps can help you find small and diverse businesses. Below are comprehensive directories and online platforms, as well as tips on how to decipher lists and bloggers' suggestions. While online tools change over time, what remains constant is how you decide which tools to use.

Be careful with online tools because they often reflect the preferences of other consumers rather than providing a selection based on a specific criterion. The diagram below shows the questions to ask yourself before trusting a source of online information.

Can You Trust Your Online Sources?

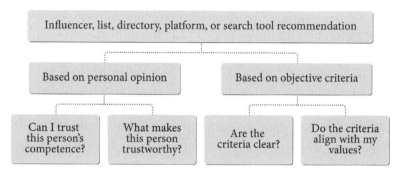

First, check if the source of information—an influencer, blog, list, or shopping directory—is based on opinion or a set of criteria. For example, I consider a list of certified women-owned businesses from the Buy Women Owned site more trustworthy than a blogger's list of favorite women's businesses, unless the blogger explains how the list was compiled and that they weren't compensated for the listing.

Most online tools provide ratings by people in your community. If your neighbor knows a great deal about gardening, their opinions about garden shops might be helpful. However, take most recommendations with a pinch of salt if you don't know anything about the reviewer. Also, most search tools do not confirm the authenticity of the reviewer, nor do they distinguish between locally owned and simply "local" shops. Nonetheless, I use them to initially find a few options and then do my own poking around to learn more about the business.

Table 6.1. Four Types of Online Tools

Based on Opinions	Based on Transparent Criteria
Lists are just that—a list of someone's favorite shops or products, usually based on opinion with no disclosed criteria.	Directories usually apply selection criteria that are maintained by an organization.
Apps such as Yelp and Trip Advisor help you find shops and businesses, with reviews based on opinions.	Online platforms, such as Etsy, sell products from a variety of smaller companies, usually with some criteria applied.

Directories that apply explicit criteria are usually maintained by an organization. For example, your local Chamber of Commerce may have a directory of businesses in your community. Directories help you find the business but do not sell products. They're often organized by location or type of business owner—local, veterans, women, Black, Indigenous, and other people of color. Each chamber is independently run, so check to see whether your local chamber produces a guide. Many cities and Chambers of Commerce publish a list of local shops for Small Business Saturday, the Saturday after Thanksgiving. All of the search tools and directories listed below are free to access, and some come as an app:

- Google or other search engines: Perhaps the easiest way to find a local shop is to search for "locally owned + type of shop + name of your town or zip code."
- Local Facebook groups: Try searching "local businesses near me."
- Nextdoor: Commonly used for finding lost cats and dogs, this app can also help you find small businesses that your

neighbors love. It includes a Neighborhood Favorites tab for leaving reviews.

- Travel apps: Developed for travel and tourism, these apps can help you find reviews for restaurants and services in your area. The apps usually mix locally owned with national chains. Trip Advisor is the largest user-generated review site, organized by cities and states.

- GettinLocal: Helps you find local restaurants, attractions, and other fun things within a specified mile radius of where you live.

- Coupons apps: These apps, such as Local Flavor, Living Social, and Groupon, present coupons for businesses near you, including restaurants, salons, clothing stores, and dentist offices. However, many national chains use the service for marketing, so it takes a bit of digging through the listings to find locally owned businesses.

- Farmers' markets: The number of farmers' markets has tripled in the last decade, and markets can now be found in every state. During the holidays, you can also find specialized markets full of locally made gifts and special treats. To find a market near you, search
  - USDA's Farmers Market Directory
  - LocalHarvest.org
  - EatWellGuide.org
  - Soko Farmers' Market app

- The Veteran Owned Business Project comprehensive directory of the small, medium-size, and large businesses owned by veterans, disabled veterans, active-duty military, reservists, and military spouses can be searched by state and category.

- Buy Women Owned is a large directory of consumer products certified by the Women's Business Enterprise National Council or WEConnect International.

- Shopbipoc.com, as the name implies, is a directory that connects you to businesses owned by Black and Indigenous people and other People of Color. The site supports individuals and business-to-business connections.

- EatOkra is a directory of almost 10,000 Black-owned restaurants in the United States.

- Support Black Owned is an extensive directory offering multiple ways to search and find user reviews.

- Black Business Green Book is a directory of Black-owned businesses that you can search by state.

- The Indian Arts and Crafts Board compiles works from Native American arts and crafts businesses and individual artists from federally recognized tribes. You'll find a wide range of jewelry, clothes, food products, and fine arts. The Arts and Crafts Board Directory saves time compared with checking individual tribe websites and marketplaces.

- The Soko Farmers' Market app provides a free listing of farmers' markets. If your local market isn't listed, you can add it to the site.

- For finding refugee-made products, Change the World by How You Shop lists a range of products and sellers. It also provides a list of businesses that support refugees, orphans, disabled people, and other vulnerable groups.

Online Shopping Platforms

Many specialized platforms sell products and services from specific types of businesses. Most are transparent about their criteria for the listings. Here are some good options:

- We Buy Black is the largest e-marketplace for Black-owned businesses.
- Pink Spot, Pride Pages, Queerly, and Gayborhood help connect consumers with LGBTQ+-friendly businesses and services.
- Etsy and Amazon enable you to sort your search to look for Black-owned, Hispanic, Asian and Pacific Islander, refugee, and LGBTQ+ Pride shops. The Indigenous Artisan Collective is an easy way to find authentic pieces.
- Etsy is also a great place to find items locally. Under the "shop location" tab, you can select "custom location" and type in your area and then filter by town, state, or country.
- Beyond Buckskin carries products from more than forty individual Native American artists. Purchasing from these platforms ensures that indigenous art is preserved, and the artists are supported directly.

Lists and Bloggers' Suggestions

Influencers are in the business of building up a social media following so that they can be paid to promote products. Skeptical about promoted products? Some influencers are genuinely passionate about their niche, such as cooking, gardening, or martial arts. They often offer valuable tips. However, others are in it for the money. In my mind, they're no better than a celebrity committing greenwashing (see Chapter 3).

Video makers and bloggers' lists—found on their own sites, YouTube, Substack, and similar places—reflect their taste and preferences. Bloggers usually don't sell products directly, but many provide links and sometimes discount codes. Unfortunately, as of this writing, there isn't a centralized source of these lists.

How can you determine which bloggers or video makers to trust? Check the person's background. Is there some reason you should trust this person's opinion? Does the person indicate how they research the products or generate their lists? Is the person paid a commission or given free products?

Tip: If the blogger or video maker includes a discount code for a product, they are most likely earning a commission. It's not necessarily a bad sign, but any lack of transparency about earning commissions is. Unsure if someone you follow earns commissions? Ask them.

Tip #4 Avoiding the Worst

Shopping online provides the least benefit to your local community compared to other shopping methods, and it frequently diverts business away from local shops. However, many small businesses thrive precisely because they can reach customers online, whether through their own websites or popular retail platforms. Use your superpower online to actively support small businesses, particularly those owned by women, veterans, and Black, indigenous, and other people of color.

Platforms like Amazon, Etsy, and Target make it easy to discover products from a diverse array of business owners. These sites allow you to filter your searches to find offerings from small businesses owned by women, Black, Hispanic, military families, Asia

Pacific Islanders, Native Americans, and LGBTQ+ individuals. For example, a simple search using the phrase "name of shopping platform + women owned business" can help you locate specific listings that support women-owned businesses.

Tip #5: Tell Brands You Care

Here are three ways you can easily give a boost to a locally owned business.

Reviews

You've found a great local cafe, restaurant, or nail salon—now leave a review so that others can find them. Online reviews are one of the best ways for you to support a business, and it doesn't cost a penny. You can write online reviews on online search tools such as Google, Yelp, and Facebook. Share photos if you have a few good snaps!

Superpower Tip: Increase the credibility of your review by stating why you like the business and something about yourself. For example, "I'm a mom of three boys and everything I've bought at Busy Bee Kidz Clothes has proven to be indestructible. Worth it!"

Bring These Businesses to Work

My colleagues in Atlanta were thrilled when the Refugee Coffee Company food truck rolled in to provide coffee at work events. It created a buzz beyond the hit of caffeine.

If you're employed, take your shopping superpower to work. Look for ways to hire the types of businesses you want to support. For example, my team negotiated with a conference venue to bring in local food vendors to give attendees an authentic taste of New

York experience. Attendees loved it, and it gave the food vendors a new deal with a major hotel.

Support your company's procurement team to source women- and minority-owned businesses. If your company needs to hire accountants, lawyers, or any type of service, ensure the search includes women- and minority-owned firms. One of my corporate clients worked with his bank to identify and hire underwriting firms with a Minority Business Enterprise (MBE) designation. Consider contracting with local coffee roasters and bakeries for the office break room, and family-run businesses for catering company meals. It makes a difference, and it's doable.

Sponsorship for Chamber of Commerce Members or Professional Networks

If you are a member of your local Chamber of Commerce or other professional networks, consider sponsoring a local woman or minority business owner. Small businesses often miss out on networking opportunities because they can't afford the fees associated with joining professional organizations. Providing a year of membership can give them a huge boost, especially if you take care to gently coach them along the way to maximize their membership benefits.

SUMMING IT UP

Your purchases from local and women- and minority-owned businesses do more than financially support the business. Most of these businesses are building something they're proud of and they want to share it with you. These business owners and small-scale producers care deeply. They do the work because it matters to them.

"The best part is, when it matters to them, it might matter even more to us. If we want to have the option of choosing something that isn't in the ordinary course of convenient and cheap, we need to show up for the people who bring it to us," explains Seth Godin.[123]

We get what we support.

Use the following summary tables as a cheat sheet to start your one change a week. These tables are structured to prompt ideas. A frequent purchase for me may be an infrequent one for you. What matters is that you try to make one switch each week.

Table 6.2. High-Impact Switches for Frequent Purchases

Item	Current Choice	Switch To
Baby Supplies	National brands bought at large chain stores online or in person	Local shops, Etsy, Shopbipoc, and other directories.
Coffee, Tea, Beer, Specialty Drinks	National-brand coffee, tea, beer, and specialty drinks such as kombucha or lemonade	Locally roasted and blended coffee and tea, including veteran roasters. Regionally brewed and made beer, cider, kombucha, and soft drinks. Women-owned, minority-owned, veteran-owned businesses. Shops owned by uncelebrated proprietors.
Coffee Shop	Chain coffee shops	Locally owned coffee shops. Use local Chamber of Commerce listings.
Eating Out	Chain restaurants, ice cream shops, or drive-thrus	Locally owned restaurants, ice cream shops, and sandwich shops. Look for ones owned by minorities and uncelebrated proprietors. Use the EatOkra directory.
Fresh Produce	National grocery stores	Farmers' markets or grocery stores that carry local produce and prepared foods. Use Soko or the USDA Farmers' Market Directory.

Table 6.2. High-Impact Switches for Frequent Purchases (Continued)

Item	Current Choice	Switch To
Meat, Bread	National brands from grocery stores	Locally owned butcher and/or baker, grocery stores that carry local meat and baked goods.
Hair and Beauty	Chain hairdressers, barbers, and beauty salons	Locally owned and women-owned hairdressers, barbers, and local beauty spas, including nail bars. For suppliers, check Shopbipoc and other directories.

Table 6.3. High-Impact Switches for Infrequent Purchases

Item	Current Choice	Switch To
Books	National chains and online	Independently owned bookstores.
Clothing, Accessories, Shoes	National chains and online	Local boutiques, consignment shops, or craft fairs. Online stores supporting charities. Check directories.
Craft Supplies	Chain craft and hobby shops such as Michael's, Hobby Lobby	Locally owned craft and hobby shops.
Eating Out	Chain restaurants	Locally owned restaurants. Look for one owned by minorities and other unsung heroes. Check local Chamber of Commerce listings and Eat Okra
Flowers, Plants, Garden Supplies	National chains, such as Home Depot	Flowers, plants, and garden supplies from a locally owned shop or farmers' markets. Look for women- and minority-owned businesses. Check local Chamber of Commerce listings.

Table 6.3. High-Impact Switches for Infrequent Purchases (Continued)

Item	Current Choice	Switch To
Gifts	Online or at national chains such as Walmart, Kohl's, Sam's Club	Gifts bought locally or online from women-owned businesses, Native American artisans, and companies supporting refugees and other unsung heroes. Use directories such as Shop-bipoc, Support Black Owned, By Black, Gayborhood, and others.
Home Furnishings	Online, department stores, specialty national retailers	Handmade by artisans, found on Etsy or in directories. Products with Nest or Goodweave certification.
Jewelry	Chain stores, online from chain stores	Handmade by artisans, found on Etsy or directories, including the Indian Arts Craft Board.
Pet Supplies	Big-box store or national chain	Locally owned pet store and groomer.

Chapter 7

HEALTH: SHOP TO AVOID POTENTIAL HEALTH HAZARDS

The products you purchase—ranging from food and cosmetics to personal care items, household cleaners, and clothing—often contain potentially harmful chemicals that pose risks to your and your family's health and well-being. You might be unaware that you're potentially exposing yourself to harmful substances in your daily life. Your diet may include foods with worrisome levels of pesticide residues. Your skin-care routine could involve applying products that contain ingredients linked to cancer. Even your household cleaning products might expose you to potentially dangerous chemicals as you scrub your sink.

This chapter is organized by category of product because the challenges in each category merit specific consideration. You'll learn how to avoid potentially toxic chemicals in your

- food
- cosmetics and personal care products
- household cleaning materials
- clothing

In the second part, you'll find tips and tools to make healthier choices for your household. The chapter only covers toxicity related to the above product categories and does not address other aspects of health. I am not a medical professional, and the following information is not intended to offer medical advice.

FOOD

It can be quite a fright to realize what's hidden in some foods. This section describes some of the risks of toxic chemicals and coloring in what you eat. The chemicals include additives such as colors, pesticides that were used on the crops, or ingredients in the manufacturing process, such as sweeteners and rising agents. The section does not address the nutritional value of foods, or the potential labor concerns and environmental impacts covered in Chapters 4 and 5.

Your Halloween Treats May Be Scarier Than You Think

Red No. 3, a coloring agent, is an ingredient found in a lot of candies. If you buy Halloween treats, the odds are that some contain Red No. 3. It is known to cause cancer and has recently been banned in the United States in food effective 2027. But in many places, it is still in food given to children.

The scientific findings about Red No. 3 and other non-banned colors such as Red No. 40, Yellow 5, and Yellow 6 are concerning. The U.S. Food and Drug Administration (FDA) found Red No. 3 to be an animal carcinogen, causing tumors in rats. Yellow 6 is known to cause tumors in kidneys and adrenal glands. A 2021 study by the California Environmental Protection Agency's Office of Environmental Health Hazard Assessment found that many synthetic food dyes, including Red No. 3, are associated with adverse neurobehavior in children. The study found links to attention-deficit/hyperactivity disorder (ADHD) and other behaviors. The good news is that you don't have to wait for 2027 for the ban on Red No. 3 or future bans on other concerning food additives. In this chapter, you'll learn what to look for on packages and how to find healthier alternatives.

Chemicals Lurk

Potentially health-harming chemicals in our food originate from three phases involved in bringing food to your table: growing, processing, and packaging.

Most conventional food is grown and raised using various chemicals, including pesticides, herbicides, animal growth hormones, and antibiotics. Some pesticides are known to be harmful to human health. The Environmental Working Group (EWG) determined that, after washing, nearly 75 percent of nonorganic fresh produce sold in the United States contained residues of pesticides. *After washing!*

During processing and packaging, preservatives and coloring agents are often added to extend shelf life and increase appeal. Not all chemicals used in food processing are dangerous to your health, but some are. For example, potassium bromate has been a food additive for the past ninety years. It strengthens bread dough and allows for higher rising in the oven. Commercial bakers use it to improve the texture of bagels, bread, and pastries. Potassium bromates cause kidney damage and cancer in laboratory animals and have been banned in California and numerous countries, including Brazil, Canada, European Union countries, and the United Kingdom. Is it in your bagel?

What Is Organic Food?

Certified organic foods—both plant- and animal-based—are free from chemicals. No added chemicals are used to grow, raise, process, or package the food. Selecting organic food is the easiest and surest way to avoid potentially harmful chemicals in your food. Organic certification indicates the foods have been grown or raised without the use of

- artificial chemicals
- hormones
- antibiotics
- genetically modified organisms (GMOs)

The food must be free from

- artificial food additives
- artificial sweeteners
- preservatives
- coloring
- flavoring
- monosodium glutamate (MSG)

Organic products, including food, cosmetics, and fibers for clothing, can be certified to four different levels:

- "100 percent organic" means what it says, and it can carry the USDA organic seal.
- "Organic" means the product contains 70 percent to 99 percent organically produced ingredients, and it can carry the USDA organic seal.

- "Organic [*name of ingredient*]" means the product contains at least 70 percent organic ingredients and can list the specific ingredients as organic, but it cannot carry the USDA organic seal.
- "Organic ingredients listed" is for products containing less than 70 percent organic contents, and it cannot carry the USDA organic seal.

"Organic" does not tell you about the working conditions of the farmers and food processors. However, it's a good proxy. It's likelier that the workers are treated fairly if the producer has gone through the effort of earning an organic certification.

Which Foods to Prioritize for Organic

Organic food isn't always easy to find and often costs more than conventional alternatives. That's why EWG's two lists—the Dirty Dozen and Clean Fifteen—are so helpful. Using USDA data, EWG ranks forty-six of the most popular fruits and vegetables according to levels of pesticides detected after washing and peeling as one would do at home. The Dirty Dozen are the fruits and vegetables with the highest pesticide contamination. These should be your priorities for buying organic or otherwise avoiding nonorganic. The Clean Fifteen is a list of the fruits and vegetables that absorb the lowest amount of pesticides and fertilizers. If you're not buying all organic, these fifteen are good choices to buy conventional produce. These two lists are updated annually. Remember to rinse your produce under running water for about twenty seconds to reduce your pesticide exposure further.

Don't use the Dirty Dozen as a reason to not eat fresh fruits and vegetables. Eating a nonorganic strawberry is a healthier choice than a strawberry-flavored gummy bear. If organic food is out of reach, focus on buying EWG's Clean Fifteen, the fruits and vegetables that come with the least pesticide exposure.

Table 7.1. The Dirty Dozen and Clean Fifteen

The 2024 Dirty Dozen	The 2024 Clean Fifteen
• strawberries	• avocados
• spinach	• sweet corn
• kale, collard, and mustard greens	• pineapples
• grapes	• onions
• peaches	• papayas
• pears	• sweet peas (frozen)
• nectarines	• eggplants
• apples	• asparagus
• bell and hot peppers	• kiwis
• cherries	• cabbages
• blueberries	• cauliflowers
• green beans	• cantaloupes
	• broccoli
	• mushrooms
	• honeydew melons

Looking Colorful?

Clean food doesn't have to be beige. FDA-approved natural food coloring includes red coloring from dehydrated beets, yellow from annatto extract, or orange from beta-carotene.

All colors—synthetic or natural—must be listed as ingredients on the nutrition label. This is important because the safety of artificial food dyes derived from petroleum is disputed. Some food dyes are deemed safe in one country but banned in another. For example, the FDA approves Green 3 as safe, but it's banned in Europe. Other colors are banned in the United States but allowed in Europe. This situation can be confusing and difficult to navigate.

Red No. 3 and Red No. 40 are known to contain carcinogenic chemicals, and there is evidence that several other dyes also are carcinogenic, cause hyperactivity in children, or provoke allergic reactions.[124]

Fishy Tales

Another source of potentially hazardous chemicals is certain fish. Mercury accumulates in ocean fish and in your body if you eat these fish. Mercury poisoning can damage your brain, nervous system, and other bodily functions. This can result in irritability, fatigue, behavioral changes, tremors, headaches, hearing and cognitive loss, and worse.[125]

How Mercury Ends Up on Your Plate

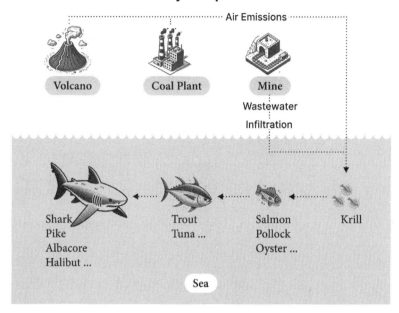

Nearly all fish and shellfish have traces of mercury. In general, small fish are eaten by larger fish. Large fish accumulate concentrations of mercury from what they've been eating, and predatory deep-ocean fish tend to contain the highest levels.[126] Tuna is the most common source of mercury exposure in the United States. The EPA recommends not more than two servings of tuna in any form each week, including canned tuna. Chilean sea bass has similarly high levels of mercury, and thus the EPA recommends not to eat it more than a few times a month.[127]

The FDA recommends you eat fish with medium levels of mercury only once a week. Stick with smaller fish and seafood such as scallops, sardines, and shrimp, which contain less mercury than their larger predators, such as bigeye tuna and swordfish.

Table 7.2. Think Small: Saltwater Fish and Seafood with Lower Mercury Levels

Anchovy	Herring	Sardines
Black Bass	Lobster	Scallops
Clam	Mackerel	Skate
Crab	Mullet	Squid
Flounder	Oyster	Tilapia
Haddock	Plaice	Wild Salmon
Hake	Pollock	Wild and U.S. Farmed Shrimp

For a full list, see the EPA guidance on Fish Advisories and Safe Eating Guidelines[128, 129] on the EPA website.

As described in Chapters 4 and 5, fishing also has social and environmental impacts. Table 7.3 provides a list of the high-risk fish and seafood species. The risks include mercury levels, environmental damage from overfishing, and labor abuse.

Table 7.3 Higher-Risk Fish

Fish and Seafood Species	High Risks of		
	Mercury	Overfishing / Environmental Damage	Labor Abuse
Atlantic Cod		XX	
Atlantic Salmon (farmed)		XX	
Bigeye Tuna	XX	X	X
Chilean Sea Bass	X	XX	
Imported Shrimp (farmed)**		XX	X

Table 7.3 Higher-Risk Fish (Continued)

Fish and Seafood Species	High Risks of:		
	Mercury	Overfishing / Environmental Damage	Labor Abuse
Imported King Crab		XX	
King Mackerel	XX		
Marlin	XX		
Octopus		X	
Orange Roughy	XX	X	
Ray		XX	
Shark	XX	XX	
Skate		XX	
Skipjack	X	X	XX
Swordfish	XX		
Tilefish	XX		
Yellowfin Tuna*	X	X	X

XX = high risk[130, 131, 132]

X = medium risk

* Pole- or small trawler–caught yellowfin tuna is okay for the environment and safe labor.

** Labor abuse is site specific. Farmed fish and shrimp from China and Bangladesh are at risk for forced labor, as are all ocean-caught fish from Chinese vessels.[133] The Thai tuna canning and shrimp peeling industry has moderate risk for forced labor.[134]

COSMETICS AND PERSONAL CARE PRODUCTS

Cosmetics don't stay put. You eat what you put on your lips, be it gloss or lip balm. Mascara and eyeliner end up in your eye with a blink. Your skin is your largest organ, and it does a great job absorbing lotions, creams, cosmetics, fragrances, and anything else you put on it.

This section covers the potential risks you face with cosmetics and personal care products that may be made with potentially harmful ingredients. Cosmetics and personal care products are made using more than 10,000 chemical ingredients, some of which are known or suspected carcinogens. Others are toxic to reproductive systems or disrupt the endocrine system.[135] Are your cosmetics safe or made with potentially dangerous ingredients?

The cosmetics and personal care industry is self-regulated in the United States. The government does not oversee the safety of cosmetics and other personal care items. Most oversight comes from a national trade association for cosmetics and personal care companies, the Personal Care Products Council. The council represents the cosmetics industry on scientific, regulatory, and legislative issues.

Skeptical about a self-regulating industry that directly impacts your health? Don't despair. Under the United States Fair Packaging and Labeling Act, cosmetics and personal care products must list ingredients. The list enables databases and organizations to identify which products contain known toxic ingredients. However, this doesn't apply to fragrances because the concoction of a scent is a trade secret. The secret ingredient of Chanel No. 5 will remain a secret.

In the absence of government regulations, two nonprofit organizations formed to educate shoppers and fight for better regulation.

First, Environmental Working Group (EWG) covers agriculture, cosmetics, bottled water, and cleaning and other products. It seeks to "close industry loopholes that pose a risk to our health and the health of our environment."[136]

Second, the Campaign for Safe Cosmetics (CSC) is an umbrella group focusing on eliminating dangerous chemicals from beauty and personal care products. It publishes a Red List of chemicals linked to cancer and other serious health risks. The Red List also covers the chemicals used in the manufacturing process that are linked to cancer and known to be carcinogenic. While these ingredients are not in the product itself, they are used during production and trace amounts are found in many products reviewed by the CSC.

In 2022, the CSC found more than 7,700 chemicals of concern in Black beauty and personal care products. It found that products marketed to Black women often contain the most toxic ingredients.[137] In response, CSC publishes a database of nontoxic Black-owned beauty products that women can trust.

EWG and CSC developed tools to identify which personal care products include toxic ingredients. You'll also find tools and databases developed by other nonprofits, as well as cosmetics companies, that are easy to use and reliable. These tools are your friends, and you'll learn about them in the next section.

Reading labels can become a headache because ingredient names are confusing. The often-quoted rule of thumb "Don't buy products with ingredients you can't pronounce" doesn't hold for cosmetics. Not all synthetic ingredients are harmful, and perfectly safe chemical and natural ingredient names can sound as off-putting as the names of toxic chemicals. For example, Vitamin E is tocopherol, a name that does not roll right off the tongue! Using tools from the

EWG, CSC, and other databases means you can find analyses of ingredient lists and trustworthy rankings without having to memorize long names.

It's worth the effort to check your cosmetics for two reasons. Even if only trace amounts of potentially harmful chemicals are used in a product, traces add up. If each of the products you use daily—including face wash, moisturizer, shampoo, and the occasional swipe of lipstick—contains a trace of toxins, your daily accumulated exposure would exceed trace amounts. Accumulation also occurs over time. You use multiple products daily, week after week, month after month. Second, why take the risk when nontoxic alternatives are easily available?

Organic Cosmetics

One way to be certain the products you purchase are toxin free is to buy organic. Organic cosmetics and body care products are made from USDA-certified organic agricultural ingredients. Qualifying organic products from other nations carry a similar certification from the country of origin. The certification requires that producers of the organic agricultural ingredients, the handlers of the ingredients, and the manufacturer of the final product all be certified as USDA Organic. Some products contain a lot of water and mineral ingredients that are never considered organic. Products can be certified to four levels, as covered in the section above about organic food.

Does going clean mean compromising on performance? No. Romy Fraser, founder of Neal's Yard Remedies and the visionary who produced and brought to market the first-ever certified organic skin and personal care products, explains, "It's very important to see beauty as part of health or an expression of health. How can a skin product that damages the environment (which we are part of) possibly 'work'? Natural ingredients are effective. Health and beauty are for the long term, it's not just expensive trickery. Skin and hair products must be effective, or we won't use them. Natural ingredients can work short-term and long-term. But we may need to adjust our expectations. We cannot, however, accept anything less than a product that fits its purpose and causes no damage."[138]

Fragrance

Fragrance is protected as a trade secret. If a product includes fragrance, it will not list the fragrance's ingredients. Fragrances are often made up of a mix of chemicals, including phthalates, solvents, and colorants. The watchwords for undisclosed ingredients are "fragrance," "perfume," and "parfum." Luckily there are "clean" fragrant solutions available, so you don't have to smell like the gym. Look for "natural fragrances," which must contain 100 percent natural and organic ingredients formulated without any synthetics.

Chemicals to Avoid

Here's a list of the nasty chemical ingredients worth avoiding. I compiled the eight ingredients below from EWG,[139] Susan Curtis and Romy Fraser,[140] and other sources as indicated. Don't worry—you don't have to memorize them. Tip #3 provides a list of tools to help you quickly find products without these and other nasties:

1. Parabens are preservatives in cosmetics. They are known endocrine disruptors. The accumulative effect of using many products at one time with one or more types of parabens is poorly understood.[141] Avoid any ingredient ending in "paraben," such as methylparaben.

2. Formaldehyde releasers do what their name implies. They slowly release into cosmetics the carcinogen formaldehyde at levels that suppress microbial growth and extend the product's shelf life. Regulators consider amounts released to be too low to wreak harm on people. Even so, look out for these releasers:

   - DMDM hydantoin (Glydant)
   - sodium hydroxymethylglycinate
   - imidazolidinyl urea (Germall 115)
   - diazolidinyl urea (Germall II)
   - tris(hydroxymethyl)nitromethane (Tris Nitro)
   - quaternium-15 (banned in the European Union)[142]

3. Phthalates make plastics soft, make nail polish stick, and help fragrance linger. Some phthalates are endocrine disruptors. Dibutyl phthalate (DBP) is used in nail polish and is listed by the European Union as an endocrine-disrupting compound of high concern. Some companies have phased DBP out of nail products. It's worth checking if your nail polish has it.

4. 1,4-dioxane is a by-product of chemical processes and a trace contaminant. It is known to cause cancer and is under review by the EPA, but such reviews can take years. To avoid 1,4-dioxane, steer away from products with polyethylene, or polyethylene glycol (PEG), and compounds that include laureth in the ingredient names, such as sodium laureth sulfate.[143]

5. Triethanolamine (TEA) is used to balance pH in cleansing creams and milks, moisturizers, eye gels, and more. It's carcinogenic in female lab mice and can be contaminated by nitrosamine, another probable human carcinogen.

6. Triclosan and triclocarbon are pesticides used for their antimicrobial properties. They're known thyroid toxins and persist in our bodies for a long time.

7. Hydroxy acids (AHAs, BHAs, lactic and glycolic acid) are not toxic but increase ultraviolet sensitivity and sunburn. They cause exfoliation, which results in the skin re-forming more tautly and makes the skin more susceptible to damage and hazards.

Animal Testing for Cosmetics Is Cruel

Animal testing, often using rabbits, is still done for many cosmetic ingredients and products. The practice is banned in many countries, including in member countries of the European Union, Mexico, and the United Kingdom. However, many of the bans have large loopholes, allowing companies to continue to use ingredients that have been tested on animals.

Most nontoxic cosmetics companies are cruelty-free. But you don't have to guess. The certifications and the Leaping Bunny app, discussed below, make it easy to check.

Toss Out Your Old Stuff

Got an old tube of mascara rolling around in your makeup bag or your favorite lip balm from two summers ago in your purse? You wouldn't wipe a moldy cloth on your face, so why use contaminated cosmetics? Preservatives help keep these in check, but over time preservatives can break down, allowing bacteria and fungi to grow. Dipping fingers into a product adds bacteria and mold, as does moisture from a bathroom environment. Take time to check the shelf life of your cosmetics and personal care products.

The expiry of cosmetics has two parts: the shelf life from the time of production and the period after you open it.

1. The average shelf life of makeup, skin care, and perfume is three to five years. In the United States, cosmetics manufacturers are not required to give expiration dates on the labels of cosmetics and personal care products. However, in Europe and many other countries, cosmetics with a shelf life of less than thirty months must be marked with a "best before" (BBE) date. Many cosmetics sold in the United States follow European Union BBE standards. For products without a BBE, you can look up batch numbers on databases, such as checkfresh.com. This is designed to work with a smartphone in a store, but some reviewers find it cumbersome.

2. The period after opening (PAO) starts when you first break open the seal of a product. The PAO is the number of months the product is still good to use after you open the package. The number is given inside the PAO logo, which shows an open lid. See below.

Period After Opening

The PAO Symbol

The period after opening (PAO) of a cosmetic product starts when you first break open the seal of a product. A number inside a drawing of an open jar indicates the PAO. It represents the number of months the product is still good to use after you open the package.

6 M

Keep It Fresh Around Your Eyes

Your eyes are most at risk. Eyelashes naturally have bacteria on them, and your mascara applicator picks up a bit of bacteria with each use. Eyeliner, eye shadow wands, and makeup brushes also collect bacteria. Inside cosmetic containers, a soup of bacteria brews that can cause eye infections or allergic reactions. For this reason, most cosmetics for eyes have a PAO of six months.

To reduce risk, don't use expired eye makeup. Be extra careful to wash your hands before and after using it. Keep the containers in a clean, dry location.

HOME CLEANING PRODUCTS

Who doesn't love the fresh smell of clean laundry?

Unfortunately, that scent may be causing you harm. Fragrances in laundry detergent, meant to impart a fresh scent, often contain an undisclosed cocktail of synthetic chemicals. These chemicals can trigger respiratory issues and allergic reactions and contribute to indoor air pollution. Some products contain chemicals associated with eye, skin, or respiratory irritation, or other human health issues.

Unfortunately, ingredient labels are not mandatory for cleaning products sold in the United States. According to the EPA, risks from chemicals in home cleaning products at typical exposure levels are often uncertain and, in many cases, assumed to be low.[144] However, home cleaning products often contain harmful substances, such as quaternary ammonium compounds (QACs or Quats), ammonia, chlorine, 1,4-dioxane, and phthalates. Some products release volatile organic compounds (VOCs). VOCs are chemicals that vaporize at room temperature. Prolonged exposure to VOCs and other chemicals may result in health problems, including respiratory illness, skin irritation, and headaches. Moreover, when these products are washed down drains or disposed of improperly, they can contribute to water pollution and harm aquatic ecosystems.

The Flow of Chemical Exposure

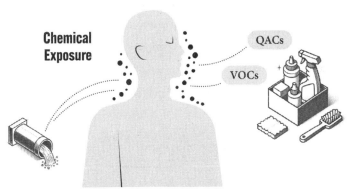

Many household products often contain potentially harmful ingredients, including

- aerosol spray products
- air fresheners
- chlorine bleach
- detergent and dishwashing liquid
- dry cleaning chemicals
- hand sanitizers
- rug and upholstery cleaners
- furniture and floor polish
- oven cleaners

That list covers just about everything most households use to clean! It can be a bit of a downer to realize that so many products might be causing harm. This is why many people advocate making your cleaning products from household ingredients such as vinegar, baking soda, lemon, and salt. But don't worry—you don't have to concoct your own products to ensure nontoxic, effective cleaning products. Many available options are safe to use, and the tips below help you identify them.

CLOTHES

Most clothes are treated with chemicals. Fabrics, threads, and accessories are dyed, and many are treated with compounds that make them fire-, odor-, stain-, water-, and wrinkle-resistant. Polyester and nylon—both fossil fuel derivatives—require a heavy chemical cocktail to produce the fine drape or rip-resistant toughness in clothes.

One of the worst offenders is PFAS, a group of chemicals known as forever chemicals because they don't biodegrade. PFAS are linked to liver cancer in humans and were recently banned from U.S. drinking water. PFAS are used for stain- and water-resistance in clothing. Rain jackets, hiking pants, sports uniforms, and school gear are often made with PFAS.

Last summer, I was planning a big hike and needed rain gear. Water-proofing a garment often involves a cocktail of potentially harmful chemicals. I dreaded looking for a jacket and pants to keep me dry without all the nasties. Luckily, finding PFAS-free rain gear was easy by looking for the certifications discussed in Tip #2 below. Despite two days of nonstop rain on the hike, I stayed dry and reached the top of the mountain.

The Federal Trade Commission requires U.S. clothing retailers to disclose fiber content, country of origin, and the manufacturer's name on the label. However, they are not required to reveal the chemicals used either in the fabrics or finishings of the garment.

Unfortunately, these chemicals may make you sick. Clothing often carries multilayered chemical profiles, built up from the weaving, dyeing, finishing, and assembly processes. These chemicals can cause asthma or skin irritation. Some are known carcinogens.[145]

Many experts think that most chemical residue on clothes is washed away with the first spin in the washing machine. Always wash your newly purchased items before wearing them—and if you get a rash, stop wearing them. Here's a list of powerful chemicals you don't want on your clothes:

- Bisphenol A (BPA) is a hormone-disrupting chemical known to cause developmental and reproductive harm and can be absorbed through our skin. Polyester clothing with spandex—such as socks, sports bras, and athletic shirts—was recently found to have a high likelihood of containing BPA.[146]

- PFAS (perfluoroalkyl and polyfluoroalkyl substances), PFCs (perfluorinated compounds), and PFOAs (perfluorooctanoic acids) are forever chemicals. These acronyms refer to fluorinated chemicals with slightly different molecular structures and similar functions. You might see these terms used interchangeably.

- Azo dyes are among the most common chemical color dyes used in clothes. They are found on almost all types of natural and synthetic fabrics. Many azo dyes are banned in the European Union and California because they are classified as carcinogens. However, at the federal level in the United States, no specific regulations ban azo dyes. Instead, some of the harsh ingredients used with azo dyes are restricted or banned. Studies of imported clothing still find unsafe levels of azo dyes in some clothing.

- Formaldehyde can cause respiratory problems and irritate skin, and at high exposure has been linked to cancer. It's sometimes used to make performance clothing wrinkle-resistant.
- Phthalates are endocrine disruptors. Some are regulated in the United States and European Union. They are used in making plastics, including polyester and PVC. They are also used to incorporate plastics into shoes and gloves.

In the section below, you'll learn how to find clothes free from potentially harmful chemicals.

What Is Organic Clothing?

Organic certification for clothes refers to how the natural fibers used to make the clothes were grown. Cotton, linen, hemp, and bamboo can be grown organically, milled into fabric, and made into clothes that carry organic certifications. A garment can be labeled organic if 95 percent of the fabric is organically grown.

"Natural fibers" does not mean organic. Natural fibers simply means that the clothing is made from nonsynthetic fibers. Natural fibers can be grown with pesticides or herbicides, unless they are also certified organic.

Theoretically, certified organic cloth can be drenched in chemical dyes because the certification only refers to how the fiber was grown. That's why certifications covered in the following section are so important. Most brands that go through the effort of sourcing certified organic fabrics maintain their natural approach and also partner with third-party certifiers and don't use potentially harmful chemicals, dyes, or finishings.

YOUR SHOPPING SUPERPOWER TIPS AND TOOLS

I love lipstick. In fact I collected a dozen or more shades—soft pink, glowing red, dusty beige, even deep purple. So when I learned that my prized collection may have been poisoning me with traces of lead, cadmium, cobalt, aluminum, titanium, manganese, chromium, copper, and nickel, I was horrified. What's more, I learned that expired lipstick can add bacteria to the toxic mix. The skin on your lips is so thin that it is vulnerable to bacteria that can build up in expired glosses, balms, and lipsticks. I threw out all of my lipsticks that were past their PAO date. Now I only buy one verified toxin-free lip color and use it up before buying another.

It's empowering to make decisions that protect your and your family's health. However, it often requires reading product ingredients—many of which appear difficult to pronounce, much less remember. That's why the section below is important. It will help you set your priorities for making changes and share trustworthy certifications and directories. These tips and tools will help you make shopping choices that reduce your exposure to potentially harmful chemicals in food, cosmetics and personal care products, household cleaning products, and clothes. A summary for easy decision-making for routine and occasional purchases appears at the end of the chapter.

Tip #1: Make One Impactful Change a Week

You can make one change weekly to your food, cosmetics and personal care products, household products, or clothing. Start changing routine purchases and then swapping out of higher-risk products (see Tip #4).

Clean Food

For routine purchases of fruits and vegetables, prioritize buying organic for those that have the highest risk of pesticides and harmful chemicals. Use the EWG's annual Dirty Dozen list of the most at-risk produce. In 2024, the most contaminated were strawberries, spinach and collards, grapes, peaches, pears, nectarines, apples, peppers, cherries, blueberries, and green beans.

Eat fish often? Canned tuna? Reduce the amount of high-mercury fish in your weekly diet. Switch to freshwater or saltwater fish and seafood with low mercury levels. See Table 7.2 for a list of fish with low risk of mercury.

For less frequent purchases, such as holiday candy, read labels and avoid food with coloring Red No. 3 and Yellow No. 6, which are known to contain carcinogenic chemicals. Check labels for the three synthetic colors banned in Europe but allowed in the United States: Orange B, Citrus Red No. 2, and FD&C Green No. 3. This green is sometimes listed as Fast Green.

Clean Cosmetics and Personal Care Products

Don't worry—you don't have to change everything in one go. Let it be a process to replace products you've finished or that have hit their expiration dates. Here's a rundown of what to replace in order of importance:

- **Skin irritations are a sign change is needed.** If a product gives you a rash, get rid of it. A rash is a sign that the product contains something that your body finds harsh or allergenic.
- **Eyes and lips are the most delicate.** You absorb and ingest what you put on your eyes and lips, so make it a priority to throw out expired eye makeup, eye cream, and any lip glosses, balms, or sticks that could be contaminated with bacteria or

degrading ingredients. When you buy new products, prioritize nontoxic eye and lip products.

- **Consider products that stay on your skin.** Check expiry
dates and PAO on products that stay on your skin: creams,
lotions, makeup, and deodorant. Replace any expired products with nontoxic ones.

- **Change out other products you regularly use.** As you finish
products, prioritize replacing them with clean alternatives, for
example, face wash, shampoo, and conditioner.

Household Cleaning Products

Fragrance and quats are easy to avoid in routinely used cleaning
products. Next time you buy a cleaning product, select one that is
fragrance free. This includes laundry detergent, dishwashing liquid,
and surface cleaners. Watch out for quats in disinfectant wipes and
antibacterial soaps. You can use regular soap and water for most
jobs. According to the Centers for Disease Control and Prevention, exposure to sodium hypochlorite—which is often referred to
as "chlorine bleach" even though it contains no elemental or free
chlorine—is linked to respiratory irritation, asthma, and other
health harms. Swap chlorine bleach for nonchlorine EWG-verified
(see below) bleach.

Clothes

When it's time to replenish your wardrobe, here are the first
changes to make to avoid clothing with a high risk of containing
potentially harmful chemicals:[147,148,149]

- Prioritize buying clothes made from natural materials, including cotton, silk, wool, hemp, linen, bamboo rayon, modal,
and lyocell.

- Don't buy clothes that smell like chemicals.
- Avoid PVC and plastics next to your skin, such as jelly shoes.
- Ensure that sporting and performance materials are bluesign, OEKO-TEX, GOTS, or organic certified (see below).
- Avoid supersaturated, ultrabright, or neon colors, unless they are bluesign or OEKO-TEX certified (see below).
- Always wash new clothing before wearing it.

If you have items of clothing that you've worn for a while yet suspect are coated with chemicals, such as old rain gear, there isn't a reason to get rid of them unless they give you a rash or make you or a family member sneeze or wheeze.

Tip #2: Seek Trustworthy Certifications

As described in Chapter 3, third-party certifications with transparent standards are generally trustworthy. While none are perfect, the certifications below will guide you to shopping choices that do not expose you and your family to potentially harmful toxins.

Food

USDA-Certified Organic

USDA-Certified Organic foods are grown and processed according to federal guidelines, which means no chemical pesticides or fertilizers. The certification also addresses soil quality, animal-raising practices, pest and weed control, and use of feed or soil additives.

All certified organic food sold in the United States must be certified by a USDA-accredited certifier. This includes imported food. Certified organic foods from Canada, the European Union, Japan,

Korea, Switzerland, and Taiwan are accredited by the USDA before they can be sold as certified organic. Only New Zealand and Israel can export organic certified products directly to the United States, without needing special USDA approval.

What products are certified? Crops, livestock, processed products, and wild crops can be certified organic. Products can use a seal depending on the percentage of their ingredients that are organic. The USDA seal "100 Percent Organic" is awarded for products with 100 percent organic ingredients. The "Organic" seal is awarded to products with a minimum of 95 percent organic ingredients, excluding salt and water.

Where will you find these labels? Due to consumer demand, organic food is found in most national grocery stores, including Walmart and Target. You may also find USDA-certified produce at your local farmers' market. Regenerative agriculture, covered in Chapter 5, is a great option for eating clean and healthy. Health-related labels for meat and eggs can direct you toward better choices. Avoid meaningless labels such as "natural" or "free range." The relevant USDA labels include

- **Certified Humane** and **Certified American Humane** standards set the minimum space requirement for animals, assure the quality of bedding material, and prohibit animals confined in cages or crates. Animals are not given growth hormones or antibiotics.
- **USDA certified grass-fed** requires animals to have unlimited outdoor access during the growing season. They can eat only grass and forage.
- **USDA cage-free eggs** require that the birds can freely roam a building, room, or enclosed area with unlimited access to food and fresh water during their production cycle.

Quality Assurance International (QAI)

You'll also see the Quality Assurance International (QAI) seal for organic foods. QAI certifies produce to the USDA standard. Some food producers work with QAI to gain USDA certification, and therefore their products can carry one or both seals.

QAI also certifies other standards, including Non-GMO, True Source Honey, Certified Plant Based, Gluten Free, Animals Raised without Antibiotics, and other standards.

Cosmetics and Personal Care Products

The list below covers robust third-party and industry-led certification programs for cosmetic products. Certification covers products, not brands, because each product has its own formulation. One brand's lipstick might be toxin free, but its eyeliner might not.

Each certification and rating system deploys its own criteria for which chemicals and other ingredients are allowed. Some are stricter than others. The chemicals and ingredients that are most screened are in one or more of three major categories: irritants or allergens, potential carcinogens, and potential endocrine disruptors. Endocrine disruptors are substances that may imitate our body's natural hormones and interfere with normal signaling of these chemical messengers.[150]

THIRD-PARTY CERTIFICATIONS

These are the most robust and trustworthy certifications.

EWG Verified

EWG Verified is an independent standard created and administered by EWG. The certification is only given to products that do not contain any ingredients on EWG's comprehensive list of unacceptable ingredients with health, ecotoxicity, or contamination concerns. The product also must meet EWG's standards for ingredient disclosure and transparency—including about fragrance ingredients. EWG ensures strict scientific standards and is transparent about its criteria and evaluations. See EWG's Skin Deep rating list and app below.

What products are certified? Over 2,300 personal care products.

Where will you find this label? On products wherever you buy cosmetics and personal care products and listed on EWG's Skin Deep website and app.

USDA Organic and FDA Certifications

USDA Organic and FDA certifications for products labeled with organic claims must comply with USDA regulations for the organic claim and FDA regulations for labeling and safety requirements for cosmetics.

What products are certified and carry the seal? Cosmetics, personal care products, and household cleaning products with 100 percent to 95 percent organic ingredients.

Where will you find this label? On products wherever you buy cosmetics, including on retail platforms specializing in natural products.

NSF

NSF, an independent public health and safety organization, develops consensus-based standards to ensure that consumers are protected from false claims. The NSF/ANSI 305 standard for personal care products containing organic ingredients covers requirements for organic ingredients, material, process, production, and labeling. The "Contains Organic Ingredients" mark on a product means that it meets stringent requirements and has gone under an independent, third-party review to verify that it contains at least 70 percent organic ingredients.

What gets certified? Body care products such as cosmetics, oral care products, moisturizers, lotions, soaps, shower gels, and bath beads.

Where will you find this label? On products at all major retailers.

COSMOS ORGANIC and COSMOS NATURAL

The COSMOS ORGANIC and COSMOS NATURAL seals signal that the cosmetics company has gone beyond using organic ingredients. The standard covers in detail all aspects of the sourcing, manufacture, marketing, and control of cosmetic products. It requires care of the environment throughout the manufacturing process, including minimizing and recycling waste. COSMOS has two levels of organic certification. COSMOS ORGANIC is more stringent than COSMOS NATURAL. The percentages required vary, depending on the amount of water and minerals commonly found in each product type. COSMOS requires that the product labels state the percentage of organic ingredients in the product. COSMOS is run by a collection of European, Australian, and Asian nonprofit organizations that certify organic products.

What products are certified? Cosmetics and personal care products, mostly brands from Europe, Australia, and Asia.

Where will you find this label? The COSMOS Standard website provides a database of products.

Leaping Bunny

The Leaping Bunny certification indicates that a product is free from animal testing. It is a comprehensive standard defined by eight national animal protection groups. Leaping Bunny does not signify that the product is free from potentially harmful ingredients. The certification is awarded to brands, not specific products.

What products are certified? Cosmetics, personal care, household products, and animal care brands.

Where will you find this label? On products at all major retailers. Leaping Bunny maintains a list of brands and retailers on its website and app (see below).

Cruelty Free

The Cruelty Free program assures that no animals were harmed in the development of personal care and beauty products. It's run by the People for the Ethical Treatment of Animals (PETA), an independent nonprofit. The certification is based solely on self-reporting.

What products are certified? Any vegan consumer products, including cosmetics and personal care products.

Where will you find this label? PETA publishes a Cruelty-Free Shopping Guide.

INDUSTRY-LED CERTIFICATIONS

These include brand collaborations ranging from specialized groups of nature-based companies to more mainstream associations such as the American Cosmetic Association.

Natrue

Natrue is the International Natural and Organic Cosmetics Association and certification. It was founded by pioneering nature-based cosmetics companies, such as Weleda and Dr. Hauschka, to ensure rigorous standards for natural and organic cosmetics. The certification is used for raw materials and finished products.

Natrue requires that all ingredients are 100 percent natural or derived from nature—meaning no synthetics, GMOs, silicones, parabens, mineral oils, or microplastics. In some products, nature-identical lab-created substances, such as pigments, minerals, and preservatives, are permitted when necessary to ensure consumer safety and the purity of ingredients. Natrue distinguishes thirteen product categories, and the criteria include environmental standards for packaging. It is overseen by an independent scientific committee and audited by an independent third-party certifier. The criteria and scoring are fully transparent, and their certified product and ingredient database is publicly available.

What products are certified? Cosmetics and personal care products.

Where will you find this label? As of 2024, more than 300 brands have certification, and more than 9,500 products and raw materials carry the Natrue Label worldwide.

Natural Products Association (NPA)

The Natural Products Association (NPA) is a trade association for "natural" products, including personal and home care. The word "natural" does not have a regulatory definition. The NPA certification requires that a product has at least 95 percent "truly natural ingredients" or ingredients that are derived from natural sources, excluding water. Ingredients must be listed as generally recognized as safe (GRAS) by the FDA and contain no residues of heavy metals or other contaminants more than tolerances set by the FDA or EPA.

American Cosmetic Association (ACA)

The American Cosmetic Association (ACA) is a corporate membership association that issues numerous certifications. To qualify for ACA certification, cosmetic products must be free of chemicals on the ACA list, which includes formaldehyde, coal tar, hydroquinone, artificial fragrances, and dyes.

ACA doesn't provide a full list of chemicals and other ingredients that are not allowed, and it doesn't report results or scoring. It is thus not possible to compare this standard with other standards or databases, such as EWG's Skin Deep.

What products are certified? Cosmetics, hair products, and oral care.

Where will you find this label? On product packaging. The ACA website has a list of the "best makeup products" of the year but does not explain how the list is compiled.

Household Cleaning Products

Some marks cover personal care and household care, so you'll find them listed here and above.

THIRD PARTY CERTIFICATIONS

EWG Verified

EWG Verified covers cosmetics, personal care, and household cleaning products. It is the most stringent and robust certification for house cleaning. See under cosmetics for more detail.

What products are certified? More than one hundred household cleaning products are certified.

Where will you find this label? On cleaning products wherever you buy them. EWG's downloadable Guide to Healthy Cleaning and app provide the full list.

MADE SAFE®

MADE SAFE is a Campaign for Safe Cosmetics partner. It verifies that products are made with safe ingredients not known or suspected to harm human health, animals, or any of the ecosystems we rely on for life. Their seal applies its Ecosystem Approach, which is a scientifically rigorous independent, third-party review that determines whether materials in a given product are made without substances that are known or suspected to be harmful to humans and the environment. This approach sets it apart from other certification systems.

What products are certified? Hundreds of household products are certified, including some household cleaning products.

Where will you find this label? On most certified products. Some companies display the seal on their website rather than on product packaging. The MADE SAFE website posts a comprehensive list of certified products and companies.

epa.gov/saferchoice

EPA Safer Choice

EPA Safer Choice certification process requires that all ingredients must meet the EPA's safety criteria for both human health and the environment, including carcinogenicity, reproductive/developmental toxicity, toxicity to aquatic life, and persistence in the environment. The EPA conducts annual audits of all certified products and periodically upgrades the standards. The criteria and process are available online at epa.gov/saferchoice.

What products are certified? About 2,000 products are certified, including cleaning products used in homes and facilities such as schools and hotels.

Where will you find this label? Look for the label on product packaging wherever you purchase home cleaning supplies. The EPA maintains a database of all certified products.

UL GREENGUARD

UL GREENGUARD certification was created to tackle indoor air pollution caused by volatile organic compounds (VOCs). The EPA and the State of Washington created the certification process, which requires products to be tested for more than 300 chemicals and prove that all VOC emissions fall beneath a set limit. The certification process is managed by a specialized, for-profit standards company, UL. It does not cover other chemicals of concern in cleaning products, only VOCs.

What products are certified? Cleaning products, furniture, electronics, mattresses, and building materials.

Where will you find this label? On products, not brands.

INDUSTRY-LED CERTIFICATIONS

Natural Products Association (NPA)

The Natural Products Association (NPA) is a trade association for "natural" product companies. It is the sister certification to the NPA's Personal Care certification. The NPA certification requires that a product has at least 95 percent ingredients that are "truly natural" or derived from natural sources, excluding water. The products must not contain ingredients for which peer-reviewed, scientific research has shown human health or environmental risk. They cannot use animal testing in development except where required by law.

What products are certified? Household cleaners, laundry detergents, and concentrated and ready-to-use hard-surface cleaners.

Where will you find this label? The NPA runs both a store locator and buyers' guide to products.

Clothing

THIRD-PARTY CERTIFICATIONS

Global Organic Textile Standard (GOTS)

The Global Organic Textile Standard (GOTS) is an international certification for organic textiles that have been made to strict environmental and social standards. It's a broader set of criteria than organic fibers. The standard includes workers' rights, requires safe and hygienic working conditions, and allows only low-impact dyes and inks. Verification is undertaken only by independent certification bodies. The certification bodies regularly audit all parties involved in the manufacturing of GOTS-certified textiles through comprehensive on-site inspections.

What products are certified and carry the seal? Organic clothing, bedding, and hygiene products.

Where will you find this label? On organic-focused brands such as Simply Organic and Beaumont Organic. See full list on the global-standard website.

OEKO-TEX Standards

The OEKO-TEX Standards are comprehensive certifications that go beyond national requirements and prohibit many nonregulated chemicals. A third-party verifies compliance, and the standards are updated annually. OEKO-TEX Standard 100 checks textiles for the presence of harmful substances. If an item of clothing has this certification on its label, you can trust that the fabric, thread, buttons, and every component has been tested for harmful substances. OEKO-TEX also has standards for leather and organic cotton. The OEKO-TEX Made in Green label includes environmental criteria in the standard.

What products are certified and carry the seal? Textiles, leather, and organic cotton.

Where will you find this label? Smaller, conscientious brands such as Girlfriend Collective, Toad & Co., and Hanna Andersson. Check the online OEKO-TEX buying guide.

bluesign®

Bluesign is probably the most used certification in the United States for ensuring chemical safety. The system takes an end-to-end supply chain approach, covering fabrics and accessories. To bear the mark, a garment must be produced from a supply chain that has been approved every step of the way. It covers worker safety, environmental impact, and resource efficiency in addition to its focus on ensuring that no harmful chemicals are used. There are two levels. Bluesign APPROVED applies to fabrics and accessories produced at system partner facilities with reduced impact on people and the planet and with bluesign APPROVED chemicals. Bluesign PRODUCT is for finished products made with bluesign APPROVED materials.

What products are certified and carry the seal? Any textile-based product, such as underwear, formal dresses, hiking gear, backpacks, and knitting yarn. It's awarded to products, not brands. The bluesign mark is becoming increasingly common among sustainable outdoor clothing brands that require performance materials.

Where will you find this label? Look for bluesign PRODUCT at top outdoor gear and apparel brands, home furnishings, and major retailers. Bluesign's website also provides a list of products, so does Amazon's bluesign listing.

TIP #3: Rating Systems, Directories, and Apps

Systems and criteria for directories tend to stay stable for three- to four-year stretches. However, apps evolve quickly, so you need to know how to assess them before blindly trusting their recommendations. When you consider using an app or database, check the following:

- Who runs it? Is it a for-profit retailer or cosmetics company trying to sell you a product?
- What are the standards and ranking criteria? Stay away from any ranking or rating system that does not clearly state how the products are assessed.

- Are the assessments verified by a third party or scientific committee?

The following are product rankings and lists based on transparent criteria. All apps are free unless otherwise stated.

Food

You can take steps to lower the toxic load of your food by using trustworthy directories and apps. The USDA's FoodData Central is the most comprehensive source of food composition data, but you need to know what you're looking for to find your way through the extensive datasets.

The Shoppers' Guide and Food Scores, both by EWG, make it simple. Based on USDA testing data, they are easy-to-use sources for all sorts of food—canned goods, baked goods, salad dressings, frozen foods, and more. The EWG database scores foods on nutrition, ingredients, and processing. You can look at the aggregate number or dig into the three individual scores. You can quickly look up baked beans, canned soup, or a package of vanilla cookies and find how they rank.

Cosmetics and Personal Care Products

TRUSTWORTHY THIRD-PARTY APPS AND DATABASES BASED ON CERTIFICATIONS

- **Skin Deep** by EWG covers cosmetics, personal care, and household cleaning product ratings. The app and website vet more than 100,000 products and provide layers of information about ingredients. An independent nonprofit, EWG is funded by grants and individual donations. It also provides Amazon links that generate revenue, but its rankings remain fully independent of Amazon.

- **The Non-Toxic Black Beauty Project** of the CSC includes a database of products made and sold by Black-owned companies. Products such as hair straighteners are often laden with toxic ingredients. All the companies listed are committed to safer beauty and personal care products, free of the toxic chemicals linked to health concerns.
- **Leaping Bunny** puts access to all Leaping Bunny certified companies in your pocket. You can scan product barcodes to check if a company is certified. You may be surprised at which brands are not certified. A great app for checking assumptions!
- **PETA** also runs an online searchable database of companies that don't test products on animals.

OTHER HELPFUL RESOURCES RUN BY NONPROFITS

- The **DeTox Me** app provides tips and a buying guide, but not an analysis or ranking of specific products. The app covers home and personal care products, food, beverages, cleaning products, children's products, and clothing. Detox Me was created by the Silent Spring Institute, a nonprofit scientific research group dedicated to women's health. It identifies chemicals linked to severe health risks, including those leading to breast cancer. Their research is funded by federal grants.
- **Clearya** is a free mobile app and browser plug-in that automatically scans cosmetics ingredients as you shop on Amazon, Sephora, Target, Walmart, iHerb, and other retailers. It's easy to use and provides alerts if there are potentially harmful ingredients in your shopping cart. It doesn't rank products and only covers products for which the online retailers provide ingredient lists.

COMMERCIAL AND FOR-PROFIT DATABASE AND APP VENTURES

The following groups generate revenue through premium memberships; others sell advertisements or products. All the apps below enable you to scan or type in barcodes or product names.

- **CosmEthics** ranks cosmetics by general safety information. You can filter for cruelty-free products. Revenue comes from premium accounts.

- **INCI Beauty** is named after the International Nomenclature Cosmetic Ingredient systems. It ranks ingredients from 1 to 20 so that you can decode your cosmetics based on the safety of the ingredients. Revenue comes from a blend of advertisements and premium accounts.

- **Paula's Choice Skin Care Ingredient Checker** is easy to use, and the database is reviewed by a science advisory board. You can upload a photo of the ingredient list straight from the product's packaging. Paula's Choice sells a full line of skin care.

- **Think Dirty** ranks cosmetics and personal care product on its 1 to 10 Dirty Meter. It's free, with its revenue generated by both premium membership and advertisements.

- **Yuka**, developed in France, ranks food and personal care products. It's free, and revenue is generated by premium memberships, not annoying advertising. It ranks over a million products based on ingredients, from risk-free to high risk.

If you just want to know what's in your products and arrive at your own conclusions about their toxin profile, you can use an ingredient checker, such as Cosmily, Skin Sort, Skin Carisma, and INCIDecoder.

Household Cleaning Products

As discussed for cosmetics, databases and apps evolve. At the time of this writing, the most robust, comprehensive app is EWG's Healthy Living.

- EWG's Healthy Living app rates more than 120,000 household, personal care, and food products, based on the same rigorous scientific research as informs its certification process. It ranks products A through F. The "EWG Verified: For Your Health" mark means the company discloses more product information than is usually provided on product labels, including about its formulations, manufacturing processes, and ingredients.

- Smart Label is a digital platform that provides more detailed product information than you'll find on a product's label. It covers household cleaning, personal care, pet, and food products. Smart Label is a project run by national brands and retailers.

- SCJohnson's transparency site covers more than 10,000 ingredients used in all its brands, including fragrance ingredients. In the United States, it is not mandatory to list known allergens in products, but SCJohnson provides a list of the 368 skin allergens that might appear in its products. This is very handy if you know which chemicals irritate your skin.

Clothing

- Eco Cult covers sustainable and nontoxic fashion, including specific shopping guides for fashion and nonfashion products that are toxin free. Some information is behind a paywall.

Tip #4 Avoid the Worst Offenders

Cleaning products are most likely the source of your highest risk of toxins. To avoid the worst, replace products with the highest likelihood of containing potentially harmful chemicals. Table 7.4 summarizes household cleaning products that usually contain potentially harmful chemicals. Change one each time you restock. Note: The health concerns listed are not comprehensive.

Table 7.4. Common Toxic Cleaning Products to Avoid

Product	Chemical of Concern	Potential Health Concern	Alternative
Air fresheners	Sodium borate	Endocrine and reproductive effects	EWG Verified or EWB A rated, essential oils
Antibacterial hand soap	Quats	See above	Soap and water
Big-brand window cleaner	2-butoxyethanol	Anemia, linked to impaired fertility, possible human carcinogen	Microfiber clothes, homemade mix of vinegar and water, EWG Verified, or EWG A rated
Bleaches	Chlorine, ammonia, and limonene in citrus-scented cleaners because the mix with bleach can create potentially dangerous air particles	Acute aquatic toxicity, skin irritation and allergies, respiratory effects	Nonchlorine bleach, EWG Verified, or EWG A rated

Table 7.4. Common Toxic Cleaning Products to Avoid (Continued)

Product	Chemical of Concern	Potential Health Concern	Alternative
Disinfectant wipes	Quaternary ammonium compounds (Quats)	Known and suspected: skin irritation, respiratory effects, reproductive toxicity, antimicrobial resistance	Soap and water
Dry cleaning	Perchloroethylene (Perc)	Likely human carcinogen	Wash at home. Find "green" or "wet" cleaners and ask if they are perc-free
Drain cleaners	Sodium hydroxide	Corrosive, can cause skin and eye irritation	EWG Verified or EWG A rated
Oven cleaners	Sodium hydroxide	Corrosive, can cause skin and eye irritation	EWG Verified or EEG A rated

Tip #5 Tell Brands You Care

This is your secret weapon. Brands care what you think and log the types of questions they receive.

If a brand you like doesn't provide sufficient information about the ingredients used, ask them! Send a message through the contact section information on the website or via social media. Remind them that you're a fan, and that you're concerned about your health and the health of the planet.

You can start your note with "I love your [*name specific product(s)*] but have a question about the ingredients." Here are questions you might ask:

- "Your website states that your products are 'clean' or 'natural' or 'healthy.' Can you please share with me how your company defines these terms?"
- "Your products smell great, but what is in the fragrance? I'd like to know the ingredients so that I can protect my health from allergens or possible harmful chemicals."
- "Do your products contain any ingredients that may be allergenic or irritating?"
- "Can you share a list of ingredients that you have decided not to include in any products for health reasons? Knowing what's not in your products is important to me."
- "Your website says your products are cruelty free. What standards do you apply?"
- [For clothes specifically:] "Is your company working toward offering certified products, such as bluesign or GOTS?"
- [For sports and outdoor gear:] "Do you have goals to reduce or phase out PFAS?"

SUMMING IT UP

Focus on one change a week. The starting list is long, so you can easily find products to switch next time you go to purchase one or more.

The first step is to download any apps before heading to the shops or any browser plug-ins you intend to use. It's hard to navigate in the store and online without these tools at the ready.

Table 7.5. High-Impact Switches for Frequent and Infrequent Purchases

Frequent Purchases	Special Occasion or Infrequent Purchases
Food	
Swap to organic for any of the fruits and vegetables on EWG's Dirty Dozen list for 2024: strawberries, spinach, kale, collard and mustard greens, peaches, pears, nectarines, apples, grapes, bell and hot peppers, cherries, blueberries, green beans.	Don't buy candy and holiday foods with Red No. 3, Red No. 40, Orange B, Citrus Red No. 2, or FD&C Green No. 3.
Swap fish with high levels of mercury for fish and seafood with lower or no levels.	
Cosmetics and Personal Care Products	
Stop using any product that causes irritations.	Swap to natural perfume, such as those based on essential oils that list all ingredients.
Swap to verified clean skin care and cosmetics for eyes and lips.	Swap to verified clean makeup, including foundation, blush, etc.
Swap to verified clean products that stay on the skin, e.g., face and body creams, deodorant.	Swap to clean hair care, either fragrance free or with natural perfumes.
Swap to verified clean nail polish and polish remover.	Toss products past their PAO date (every three, six, or twelve months), starting with lip and eye products.
Home Cleaning Products	
Swap to fragrance-free cleaning products.	Switch big-brand window cleaner to nontoxic cleaners.
Swap to fragrance-free laundry products.	Ask for nontoxic dry cleaning and switch cleaners if necessary.
Swap chlorine bleach to nonchlorine bleach and EWG Verified bleaches.	Switch to nontoxic oven cleaners.

Table 7.5. High-Impact Switches for Frequent and Infrequent Purchases (Continued)

Frequent Purchases	Special Occasion or Infrequent Purchases
Home Cleaning Products	
Swap to disinfectant wipes for soap and water.	Switch to nontoxic drain cleaners.
Swap antibacterial hand soap for regular soap.	Switch to nontoxic air fresheners or use pure essential oils.
Clothing	
Avoid cheap knockoffs and fast fashion.	Buy pieces that last.
Avoid any clothes that smell like chemicals.	Look for clothes made in natural fibers: linen, wool, cotton, silk, bamboo, lyocell.
Avoid anything made from PVCs and plastics that touch your body, e.g., jelly sandals.	Avoid outdoor wear and sports gear with PFAS or supersaturated, ultrabright colors unless they are bluesign, OEKO-TEX, GOTS, or organic certified.

Chapter 8

KEEP COSTS DOWN

Most shoppers say higher prices prevent them from buying sustainable and ethical products.[151] The price is a big issue, and one worth investigating. The true costs of shopping with your values can be nuanced, and in some instances, shopping this way may save you money.

In the first part of this chapter, you'll learn about

- why some sustainable products are more expensive than alternatives
- trade-offs of time and convenience
- lifetime value as a better way to consider cost
- how to consider up-front costs

In the second section, you'll find tips on how to keep costs down across a range of products.

WHY ETHICAL AND SUSTAINABLE GOODS ARE OFTEN PRICED HIGHER THAN ALTERNATIVES

Using fair labor, environmentally friendly production, and sustainable materials drives higher expenses than less scrupulous business practices. For example, paying fair wages is more costly than exploiting workers. As a result, the cost basis for a fair labor T-shirt, football, set of sheets, or pound of coffee is higher than that for similar products sold by less ethical brands.

Environmentally responsible companies often face higher production costs and more expensive raw materials than their less eco-concerned competitors. In general, it's less expensive for a company to pollute, deforest, ignore waste, and make no efforts to reduce greenhouse gases than to produce in a way that effectively reduces its environmental impact. For example:

- Recycling paper costs more than cutting down new trees and using them for pulp, so paper goods with recycled content may cost more than those with virgin pulp.
- Organic cotton and other crops are more labor, intensive and, therefore, more expensive than conventional crops, which rely on many chemical pesticides. This means most organic clothing, linens, and foods cost more than nonorganic.
- Plant-based and natural materials are more expensive than synthetics and chemicals, so items made with plant dyes and natural fibers, such as wool, linen, and cotton, cost more than those made with polyester and dyed with chemical colors.

Durability also plays a role. Making a reusable product requires using more durable materials and more design considerations than producing a single-use throwaway one, which can add to costs. Manufacturing clothes, toys, furniture, and other household goods so that they last also usually comes with higher labor and production costs. Toxin-free cosmetics, clothes, and household cleaning products require more expensive ingredients than a cocktail of chemical solutions.

However, ethical and sustainable products are only sometimes more expensive. For example, I compared the price of three similar organic cocoa crisp cereals at my local health food shop and grocery store. One was USDA Organic Certified and Fair Trade Certified; two were USDA Organic Certified but had no fair labor certification. The organic Fair Trade Certified cereal was less expensive than the other without fair labor certification. Clearly, pricing doesn't always reflect different labor costs. Branding plays a significant role.

When an environmentally friendly, fair labor or toxin-free product is more expensive, the price difference is often negligible. One reason is growth in the market. As ethical and sustainable goods become more common, price differences are diminishing, such as for organic groceries and other sustainable staple items. In 2023, New York University's Stern Center for Sustainable Business found that sustainable products are more than 18 percent of the total market, up by 5 percent since 2015. Inflation in recent years has not diminished the growth in sustainable products. The growth in volume helps bring down prices.

Accessibility and Time

Accessibility, not just price, is a barrier for too many people. Some rural and urban communities are food deserts with few alternatives. If you are in an area with few in-person shopping options, consider bulk-purchasing dry goods with your neighbors and talking to your local stores about what items you'd like to see made available.

Trade-offs in convenience and time are also necessary. Initially, it will take longer to find products that align with your values. However, once you've researched and know which brands you trust, restocking or quickly finding new products becomes fast and easy.

How do you weigh the inevitable trade-offs—for example, the trade-off of convenience against commitments to reduce plastics and disposable items? Do you buy a plastic box of salad or a head of lettuce that requires washing and chopping at home? Time is another trade-off.

Lifetime Value—a Better Way to Consider Costs

The price of an item is not the only way to determine its cost. While initially more expensive, sustainable products often offer better long-term value because of:

- higher quality and better durability, reducing replacement frequency
- energy and resource efficiency, potentially lowering ongoing costs
- health benefits from using nontoxic materials

A product's lifetime use, operating, and maintenance costs can make a less expensive item cost more over its lifespan. For example, a ten-dollar T-shirt that falls apart after five wearings is more expensive per wearing than a seventy-dollar shirt that lasts five years and fifty wears. The same holds for toys, accessories, home furnishings, and other household items. When you see a big price difference and feel tempted by the lower-priced good, ask yourself: *Is it durable? Will I use it for years to come? If it breaks, can it be repaired? Will it enable me to buy less over time?*

Here's another example. Last spring, I needed to replace my dishwasher. Water usage in washing machines varies greatly, even among the top energy-conserving machines. Standard machines use about ten gallons of water a load while water-saving machines use two gallons. A big difference! If you live in a water-stressed area, choosing a machine that has top energy ratings and uses the least amount of water may be advantageous. The price was about 50 percent more than the average dishwasher. Will I earn back some of the price difference through savings on my electric and water bills? Yes. It will save me about $60 on electricity and $20 on my water bill yearly. The emotional savings are also significant. Living in a water-stressed environment, it is a relief to have an ultra-efficient machine. It's my little badge of honor in the kitchen.

Another hidden benefit is the reduction of exposure to potentially harmful chemicals over the product's use and buildup over your lifetime. By swapping to clean cosmetics and house-cleaning products, you're reducing not only your exposure today but also the cumulative effect over your lifetime.

Myth Buster: Does Shopping Local Cost More?

It depends.

Farmers' markets and shops that sell local produce don't pay warehouse fees or delivery and shipping costs. This often results in prices that are competitive with large-scale chains. However, for many locally made items, producing in smaller quantities typically incurs higher costs than mass-produced goods. A locally made doughnut is more expensive than one from a multipack at the grocery store. Wages also can mean a difference in prices. Local shops often pay higher wages than big-box stores.

Sometimes I pay more for local foods and other items than at a big-box, grocery, or online store—but not always. I don't pay more for locally roasted coffee, high-quality tea, or in-season vegetables. I do pay more for eggs, bread, and honey at the farmers' market than I would at a grocery store. For me, it's worth the higher price because they are fresh and organic and taste better.

The price of clothing varies so much that it's hard to say if it's more expensive to buy online or at a local boutique. I pay more for craft materials at a local shop. However, I get the exact amount of materials needed, creating no waste. The price difference at the end of the project is minimal, if any. I've found board games, home decorations, toys, books, and similar items to be about the same price in local shops as they are online.

No matter the price difference, buying local gives you the feel-good factor of connecting with local businesses and helping to build a stronger community. All other things being equal, I continue to choose community over convenience.

Up-front Costs

While there are ways to cut costs, some items will require budgeting and accepting trade-offs. Buying sustainable products—especially larger-ticket items such as appliances, home furnishings, and wardrobe staples such as coats and jackets—can require more up-front investments than less sustainable options. The more sustainable and long-lasting choice may pay off over the long run. However, freeing up the cash to invest when needed is not always feasible, especially when it's an emergency purchase.

In this situation, get clear about your priorities and trade-offs. Where else might you make headway? Where can you have maximum impact for less investment? For example, if you care about climate change but the ultra-efficient washing machine is out of reach, buy the most energy-efficient one within your budget. Match it with a detergent that allows you to wash everything—no matter how dirty—in cold water. Or maybe this year, get a conventional pine table for the living room and save up for a Forest Stewardship Council–certified wooden desk for your office. Remember that your priorities are at the heart of your shopping decisions—and trade-offs, budgeting, and patience are interlaced into this new way of shopping.

As Your Shopping Habits Change, So Do Your Expenses

You may buy less as you start to focus on health and durability. For example, as you begin to pay attention to reducing your chemical exposure, you may shift to buying fewer cosmetics. I buy fewer cosmetics now because I want to finish the product before it expires. I realized that having three or four face creams open simultaneously is a waste of money because I can't use them up before the PAO date. It's better to use cosmetics sequentially, finishing a jar or tube before breaking the seal on the next. Understanding the risk of contamination from out-of-date products helps keep me immune to marketing and the allure of buying the latest colors or creams. At the end of the year, I found that I'd spent less and enjoyed my products more. Extra bonus: less clutter in my bathroom!

As you grow confident in making choices that align with your values, you may notice a shift in how you relate to your belongings.

You may decide to wait and save for items. It takes patience to save. Keep track of the changes and keep going. And remember, delayed gratification raises your dopamine level.

TIPS ON KEEPING COSTS DOWN

Below are tips on keeping costs under control while making impactful shopping choices. For some items, such as groceries and household goods, there are often workarounds to find reasonably priced, sustainable, ethical, and local products. However, there is often a more noticeable price difference for more significant items—a sweater, an office chair, or a nice gift for someone. The tips can help in both cases.

Start with Low-Cost Items Because Any Price Differential Will Be Small in Real Terms

Food is an excellent place to start because there are many switches you can make that don't necessarily cost more—or cost minimally more. For example, the current price premium for forest-friendly, Fair Trade Certified chocolate compared to a conventional big-brand bar of chocolate at my local grocery store is 22 percent. While that may sound like a lot, it is not in absolute terms. Will you spend $0.60 more for a 3.5-ounce chocolate bar made with fair labor? Similarly, organic and fair labor fruit, vegetables, and dried goods are great switches at no or little price difference.

Look for Brands That Do Not Pass on the Extra Cost to the Shopper

Not all retailers pass along the extra cost of fair labor or environmental performance products. Some retailers keep prices the same as other products they sell that are conventional or not certi-fied. Why? Companies see investing in fair wages, organic materials, or environmental efficiencies as the right thing to do and a way to grow market share. It's part of the company's value system as well as growth plan. For example, Target, Eileen Fisher, and Madewell do not charge a premium for Fair Trade Certified jeans, sweaters, and shirts. These brands have chosen not to pass on the extra cost to the shopper. Madewell, a brand owned by the J. Crew Group, is well on its way to achieving its goal of having 90 percent of its denim Fair Trade Certified by 2025.[152] The brand makes many other products, and fair labor practices seem to be baked into the company's com-mercial strategy.

Many brands choose to pass along the extra cost because they don't currently have the vision of producing mostly fair-labor prod-ucts. A brand may test the waters with a few certified product lines and, in doing so, test price points to see which will attract customers.

Work the Apps and Platforms

Some apps, such as Good On You, and online retailers, such as Amazon and Etsy, allow you to set filters on price so that only products in your budget range are displayed. This helps to avoid the disappointment of choosing something outside of your budget. For cosmetics and personal care products, apps such as Clearya can help you find clean products online and in-store at drugstores, grocery stores, and other retailers that often have lower base prices.

Buy to Last

Fast fashion is designed to quickly fall apart. Buy for life. As de-scribed earlier, consider the total cost of the product's life. Will the less expensive version last as long, or will I need to replace it in a year or two? Usually, it's less costly over five years to buy a more durable, efficient item that lasts longer.

Transition from Fast Fashion

Find durable clothes that really work for you. Well-made clothes can last a decade or more. Stains on my sports or outdoor gear? They are a badge of pride because they show they have been used outdoors.

Consider Secondhand, Renting, and Swapping

As you'll read in Chapter 9, renting, borrowing, buying secondhand, and swapping items are great ways to defray costs while reducing your environmental footprint and helping to ensure that products have longer lives. If wearing designer clothing and accessories is important to you, or if you have a fancy event to dress for, renting, swapping, and buying secondhand can offer you a large discount to get the same look as owning. Also consider keeping costs down on tools, toys, books, furniture, and small appliances by renting or swapping.

Source Food Well

To save money, look to buy specific ingredients from different stores. For example, seek out shops that sell bulk dry goods. Buy produce in-season at farmers' markets, or if not, buy frozen in grocery stores. Look for stores that sell imperfect or "ugly" foods. Nutrition matters more than appearance. Focus on the EWG's Dirty Dozen list as priority organic purchases and deprioritize buying organic for the EWG's Clean Fifteen list. For fish, think small. Anchovies and sardines are usually priced much lower than tilapia or salmon. These smaller fish are very healthy to eat, with very high levels of omega-3s and calcium and no accumulated mercury.

For Household Cleaning Products, Consider Making Your Own

Many experts recommend making simple cleaners from vinegar, baking soda, lemon, and some elbow grease. You'll find many recipes online and in books.[153] Others recommend buying a general-purpose cleaner rather than specialized products to keep costs down. And remember, always use cleaning products only as directed on the label for safe exposure levels. Dispose of the products and containers properly.

Chapter 9

SHOP NEW WAYS

Imagine having access to the latest fashion trends and high-quality tools without buying them. Next, imagine a world where everything we use is part of a continuous loop, where resources are reused, waste is minimized, and products are designed to last. You don't have to imagine these scenarios; both are here already.

They are nascent options but growing rapidly. It's cause for cheer. In this chapter, you'll learn about

- the opportunities of the shared economy for rental, repair, and resale options
- closed-loop models that greatly reduce waste and material use
- upcycling and direct-from-farm options that can help further reduce environmental impacts

THE SHARING ECONOMY

One option to reduce your costs while accessing sustainable items is to share. Just like you learned in kindergarten, sharing is a beautiful thing. It can save money and time, and even generate an income stream.

The sharing economy means that you rent or borrow an item rather than purchase it. For example, you can rent various high-quality, fashionable items for a fraction of the retail price. Renting eliminates the need for frequent wardrobe updates or buying a dress you'll wear only once to your friend's wedding. It can also be convenient, with options for delivery, return shipping, and professional cleaning. Similarly, renting tools, baby gear, garden equipment, and other items when you need them can help you avoid the substantial expense of buying something new. You can rent from your peers, companies, and nonprofits.

Peer-to-Peer Rentals

Think of it like Airbnb for your things. In peer-to-peer models, you can borrow items and loan out items you own. For example, gardening tools you need once a year or baby equipment your child has outgrown are assets you can turn into rental items, helping your neighbors get what they need and generating a bit of income for yourself. It's an exciting way to turn your closet or toolshed into an income stream and to gain access to someone else's treasures.

In recent years, several virtual peer-to-peer marketplaces, such as SIB-app and Fat Llama, have emerged to facilitate the short-term rental of durable goods. You'll find all sorts of things to lend that linger in your closets and your garage. The original model was based on location, meaning exchanges happened in person within driving distance. Today, many platforms include shipping options, so you can rent and lend with peers at a distance.

Peer-to-peer rentals are not just about the lending and borrowing of items; they're also about the community. On most of these platforms, you set the terms and make direct exchanges with other members. For example, By Rotation is a community of people who love their clothes and relish renting them directly to other members. The members negotiate prices and terms directly with one another. Friendships form online, and there is palpable excitement about seeing one another appreciating the other's beautiful pieces. Members also cheer one another on as they meet their income goals. Imagine the feeling of renting a party dress from someone saving for college versus renting from a company. It's a community built on trust and shared interests, and it's one you can be part of.

Rental Companies and Nonprofits

Traditional rental is well established in many categories, such as tools and party furnishings. It's exploding in fashion. Company-to-shopper platforms such as Nully, Rent the Runway, and Pickle are skyrocketing in growth as more people use them as an alternative to buying new fashion pieces. Some are subscription based, meaning they send you a set number of pieces monthly. You wear them, then return them. Dry cleaning and shipping fees are included in the rental price.

Look for the sustainable fashion selection on rental platforms. Many friends use these services for their daily work wardrobe, even while working from home. Lots of great shirts from sustainable fashion brands are rented. Skirts and pants not so much.

Like a library for books, nonprofit tool libraries offer free access to community members. They typically offer various items, from gardening tools and power drills to kitchen appliances and outdoor gear. Similarly, other community lending programs might include seed libraries, where members can borrow and exchange seeds for gardening, or toy libraries that provide access to toys and games for children. These programs enhance your community by encouraging you to meet and collaborate with your neighbors. They also provide low-pressure opportunities for skill sharing. Sharing libraries embody the ethos of the sharing economy.

Sometimes tool libraries appear in local town or city libraries. Can't find something near you? LocalTools.org helps you find a nearby tool library.

Repair

Repair services can extend the life of your belongings. Whether it's clothing, electronics, or toys, companies are increasingly providing repair services to extend the life of their items. Repairing helps you save money and lightens the environmental impact: no disposal, no new purchase.

Repair cafes are free meeting places to repair things such as clothes, furniture, electrical appliances, bicycles, crockery, appliances, toys, and garden equipment. You'll find tools and materials to help you make any repairs you need, and often someone with expertise to either do the job for you or show you how. They are nonprofit, free services offered by people in your community. A worldwide movement, repaircafe.org, provides a listing of repair sites around the world. If your community isn't on the list, ask at your local library.

Specialized community bicycle repair centers and cooperatives, such as Sopo Bikes in Atlanta or Kickstand in Raleigh, welcome everyone from professional bike mechanics to newbies to work together to repair their own and donated bikes. Most request a minimal donation to keep the place open and stocked with parts and tools.

Companies with a strong sustainability ethos also offer repair. Many outdoors equipment makers and retailers—such as North Face, Patagonia, and REI—offer repairs, as do forward-looking fashion companies, such as Timbuk2, IKEA, Eileen Fisher, Dyson, Levi's, Nudie Jeans, and 4 Objects. By promoting repairs, companies are gently encouraging a mindset that values longevity and sustainability.

Resale

Resale isn't new. Every town has a consignment shop of some sort. Yet since the COVID-19 pandemic, the resale market has grown due to a remarkable shift in shopping behavior. Facebook Marketplace has over 8 million monthly users in the United States. Marketplace and other platforms such as Buy Nothing Project and Nextdoor help you swap goods within your community. These platforms foster a grassroots circular economy, keeping goods in use longer and helping families avoid undue expenses.

Commercial platforms are also booming. Platforms such as the RealReal and ThredUp have reported tremendous surges in fashion sales. Amazon runs a Renewed site for gently used items. Fall in love with something you've rented? Most rental platforms also provide options for buying what you've rented.

NEW BUSINESS MODELS: CIRCULAR, CLOSED LOOP, UPCYCLING, DIRECT FROM FARM

Business models are the engines of companies. They shape how a company makes money. Most business models are linear and follow a "take-make-dispose" path. A company takes a resource, makes a product, and that product is disposed of at the end of its use. The company is rewarded for selling more products. Circular and upcycling business models follow a circular model of take-make-collect-reuse-make-collect-reuse again and again.

Closed-Loop Production, Upcycling, and Farm-to-Consumer

Closed-loop production seeks to keep materials in use for as long as possible, extract maximum value from them while in use, then recover and regenerate products and materials at the end of their service life. One example is how milk used to be sold in refillable bottles, delivered door-to-door. The glass was used until it started to chip, at which point it was recycled into something else.

The goal is to keep materials in use in their highest-value form, so a plastic container remains a plastic container for as long as possible before the plastic is turned into a molded park bench. Think of empty ink cartridges from your printer. Send them back and get them refilled at a discounted price. The plastic in the ink cartridges isn't melted down. It's kept in its higher-value form of an ink cartridge. This differs from recycling because the materials go back into the making of the same product. The system depends on you returning the material to be reused.

As a shopper in a closed-loop system, you are also a supplier. You are part of the value chain that enables more products to be made. It's your role to return packaging or components of the products after use. Companies offering closed-loop products often provide incentives for returns, such as discounts on future purchases or loyalty points.

Closed-Loop Production

In the diagram above, you see that virgin cotton is introduced into the cycle to kick off production of a dress. The dress is made, retailed, and sold to a shopper. The shopper wears the dress and, whenever they are ready to dispose of it, they drop it off at a collection site. The collection company then sorts the items. Clothing in good order is repaired and sold as secondhand. Items that are damaged are either turned into rags or the cotton fibers are harvested to make more dresses. The cotton in the dress can be used again and again, reducing the amount of virgin cotton required.

Many brands such as North Face, Patagonia, and H&M have their own collection sites. Others partner with take-back companies, such as Trashie.io. If your brand of clothes doesn't accept take-backs, you can buy a take-back bag from a company such as TerraCycle, Waste Management, or Ridwell, and send unwanted items to be sorted, upcycled, or recycled so that none of your clothes end up in a landfill. Most take-back services have specialized programs for batteries, paints, and light bulbs, as well as textiles.

More and more products are entering into closed-loop or circular systems. Grocery stores in France and other countries are leading the next generation of circularity. Evian and Badoit, two French water brands, along with a local brand, Lorina, introduced returning bottles for refill at certain large retailers in France. Many big brands such as Coca-Cola have stated intentions to develop return programs for containers.

Closed loop is a growing force for better management of household purchases. Closed-loop systems help to conserve natural resources by reducing the need for new raw materials. The number of products integrated into circular production is expected to increase significantly in the next few years, so you can jump in now to help these powerful approaches grow.

Upcycling

Upcycling is a twist on circularity and recycling. It takes a product no longer in use and gives it a second life and new function that is of higher value than the original product. People who sew have practiced this for decades: fabric scraps, such as old shirts and ties, make fabulous new items, including quilts and wall hangings. Now, innovative companies are finding ways to upcycle waste materials and give them a second life of increased value. For example, Eileen Fisher turns its fabric scraps into West Elm cushions. Clothing shop Re/Done upcycles jeans, collectibles, and recycled tees into fashion-forward pieces. If you don't sew or craft, look for upcycled products from dedicated fashion, home furnishings, and design-oriented companies.

Direct-from-Farm Model

You've probably seen farm-to-table restaurants, bean-to-bar chocolate, single-source coffee, and similar food products that help create more value for the farmer by assuring the exact provenance of the product. Often these models help the farmers better maintain and restore their land because they earn more by cutting out the middle market and selling directly to the coffee roaster, restaurant, or you, the shopper. This practice often allows farmers to maintain family farms and restore land through regenerative practices.

Similarly, farm-to-wardrobe production supports cotton and wool producers. Groups such as Nativa ensure that wool and cotton for fashion brands are sourced from farms that practice regenerative agriculture with the highest standards for fair labor and animal husbandry. Hangtags on products are marked with the Nativa logo and include a QR code that you can scan to discover the full journey of the item, tracking every step of the way—from farm to brand. With increased traceability, fashion companies and shoppers like you can be assured that your clothes are made from regenerative materials. See Chapter 5 on regenerative practices.

SUMMING IT UP

New models are all the rage, but still minuscule. Despite recent growth and attention in social media, resale and rental are less than 4 percent of the global fashion market. Textile production has doubled in the last fifteen years, yet the length of time clothes are worn has dropped 40 percent.[154] Most shoppers wear a piece of clothing such as a shirt or sweater between three and seven times.[155]

To boost the growth in these new business models, the Ellen MacArthur Foundation launched a coalition of fashion businesses—including fast-fashion giants Primark, the H&M Group, and Reformation—that commit to replacing a portion of their revenue stream from selling new goods with income from circular business models that rent, resell, and repair.

Where to Start

We're not locked into our current system of buy-use-dispose-buy again. Your shopping superpower enables you to experiment with these new ways of shopping. Try a rental for an item you know you'll only use for a short time. Start with a low-bar item such as getting your bike fixed or borrowing a garden tool at a local tool library. See how it feels. Then try something new.

Chapter 10

CONCLUSION: SHOP AS A FORCE FOR GOOD

Your power as a consumer is a force for good. Now you have the insights and tools to unleash your shopping superpower and positively impact people, the planet, and your health. You can choose to do so with each purchase you make.

Your purchasing decisions are consequential, although it may not always feel that way. In our market economy, consumer demand drives what companies sell. With each tap or swipe of your credit card, you're not only acquiring goods, but you're also shaping the economic landscape. Deploying your shopping superpower tells the marketplace that you want products that are more ethically made and environmentally sound, and businesses that support your community and your well-being. It's a subtle yet potent form of activism because every dollar you spend becomes a vote for positive change.

Products marketed as sustainable are expected to grow almost six times faster than those that are not, and the market value of sustainable fashion is set to double within six years—all because of increased demand from shoppers like you.

Unleashing your shopping superpower also enhances your happiness. It aligns your actions with your values, fostering your sense of fulfillment and purpose. You're no longer at the mercy of a dopamine rush when you see a sale, no longer fooled by the wiles of greenwashing. You exercise agency when you buy products that reflect the type of world you want. This shift enhances your happiness and contributes to a positive ripple effect, encouraging others to follow suit.

But where do you begin when there's a labyrinth of options and choices? It can feel overwhelming. In the last few years, more ethical and sustainable products have been brought to market because shoppers want them. However, since most goods on retailers' shelves—online and in shops—are not sustainable, the harmful production methods described in this book continue.

Your journey starts small, with a simple realization: Habits form by making small changes and repeating them, week after week. Focus on one change a week. This pace will slowly create shopping habits that relieve any sense of feeling overwhelmed because you have a plan, and you're taking manageable steps.

Here's a riddle: Most shoppers of all ages say they want more sustainable, ethical, and healthful options, yet only a tiny minority consistently follow through with their purchases. How can this be fixed?

One purchase at a time.

Make your first switch this week, and another switch next week.

Embrace your shopping superpower, and your purchases will better your world.

SUMMARY OF PRIORITY SWITCHES TO MAKE

There is no one-size-fits-all approach to ethical shopping. Your values, priorities, and preferences are unique, so it's essential to start where your heart leads.

Focus on one change a week. Keep going. As your new habits build over time, so will your confidence and contentment with what you buy.

Where to start? Here's a cheat sheet of suggested changes.

People

✓ Switch to certified fair labor products, starting with coffee, tea, bananas, chocolate, sugar, and other imported fruits, vegetables, and shelf items.

✓ Avoid mica in beauty products, unless the company is convincingly committed to ethical sourcing.

✓ Buy certified fair labor rugs, home furnishings, jewelry, and leather.

✓ Ask for and buy certified fair-trade jeans and other clothes at major retailers.

Planet

✓ Stop buying single-use plastics and disposable containers.

✓ Buy to last. Break up with fast fashion.

✓ Avoid anything with palm oil unless you know the company is committed to sourcing only sustainable palm oil.

✓ Buy regenerative agricultural products.

✓ Support slow-food producers, restaurants, and cafes.

✓ Support grocery stores that sign pledges to support biodiversity by banning their suppliers from using harmful pesticides.

Community

✓ Frequent your independently owned local cafes, restaurants, bookstores, hair salons, barbers, and gift shops. Tell your neighbors and write reviews.

✓ Search out women-owned, minority-owned, and veteran-owned businesses online and in your community. Find a gem? Tell your friends and write reviews.

✓ Look for gifts and special items at shops owned by or that employ refugees, people with disabilities, women, veterans, minorities, and other uncelebrated proprietors. Share the love and write reviews.

Health

✓ Switch to organic fruits and vegetables on EWG's Dirty Dozen list.

✓ Ditch foods with Red No. 3, Red No. 40, Orange B, Citrus Red No. 2, and FD&C Green No. 3.

✓ Swap big fish with high levels of mercury for smaller fish and seafood that have low levels of mercury.

✓ Don't buy new outdoor and sports gear with PFAS or items made from PVCs and plastics that touch your skin.

✓ Switch to fragrance-free cleaning products and those with good scores from EWG's Guide to Healthy Cleaning or other trustworthy ratings.

✓ Starting with products for eyes, lips, and face:

    ✓ Switch to clean beauty products that are organic or rated well by EWG, CSC, or other ratings.

    ✓ Replace cosmetics and personal care products that are past their PAO date.

RESOURCES AND TOOLS

You've found many tips, tools, and resources in this book. Here's a quick cheat sheet of my favorite go-tos:

✓ Chocolate Score Card, which rates small, medium-size, and large chocolate brands and retailers across five environmental and social criteria, including deforestation and child labor.

✓ Remake's annual accountability report, which assesses fifty-two fashion companies and rates their performance on human rights and environmental, economic, and political issues on eighty-eight individual metrics.

✓ Environmental Working Group (EWG) Skin Deep, Dirty Dozen, Clean Fifteen, and other consumer guides. Campaign for Safe Cosmetics (CSC) consumer guides.

✓ Eco Cult's resources include many pragmatic sustainable and toxin-free tips on free, as well as a for-fee, sustainable fashion guide.

✓ Third-party certified products for most everyday purchases, including Fair Trade Certified, Rainforest Alliance Certified, Global Organic Textile Standard (GOTS), Forest Stewardship Council, Marine Stewardship Council, EWG Verified, Green Seal, and USDA Organic. Review the relevant chapters and make your own list.

✓ Specialized shopping platforms, including We Buy Black, Black and Green, American Indian Food Market, Gender Fair, as well as Etsy, Target, and Amazon pages for specific types of business, including Hispanic-owned, Black-owned, and women-owned.

✓ ENERGY STAR ratings for thousands of appliances, independently certified to meet strict standards for energy efficiency.

✓ B Corporations, commonly called B Corps, are certified to meet rigorous standards of social and environmental performance, accountability, and transparency and integrate sustainability into the core of the business.

What are your go-to resources?

Share with me at dianeosgood.com and we can start a conversation.

UNLEASH YOUR SHOPPING SUPERPOWER

It's easy to go about our busy lives, prioritizing convenience, price, and Instagram-able looks when we shop. Shopping with your core values at the center of your decision-making can be so much more rewarding. It takes patience and a bit of courage, but it's essential. It's essential for the health and well-being of you, your family, your community, the people who make your things, and the planet.

You, together with shoppers all over the country, can send a signal through the marketplace that you no longer accept that workers are poorly treated or abused, that the environment is degraded, that local and minority-owned businesses struggle, and that our families' health is at risk. You'll signal that you want more products that generate better jobs for more people, restore the environment, build up communities, and help your family thrive.

Be insistent, yet don't get caught up on perfection. Remember, progress isn't a handful of people shopping with their values perfectly. It is millions of people doing it imperfectly, together making a big difference in the world.

Unleash your shopping superpower. Now in a world that seems to have lost heart, you can shop with yours.

For more in-depth information:

For free resources including tools, directories, and videos, see:

Appendix

FIND THE INFORMATION YOU'RE LOOKING FOR ON COMPANY WEBSITES

Here you'll find what to look for on a company's websites for its progress on how it:

- manages its environmental impact and improvement goals
- reduces risks of labor abuse in its supply chains
- transparently reports on health-related issues and toxicity in ingredients
- supports a diverse workforce

WHAT TO LOOK FOR

If you can't find enough information about a product on its package or from a rating app, check out the company's website. It takes a bit of time, but it will help you get a good grasp of what the company is doing to protect workers, the environment, and your health. It will also provide insights into how the company manages diversity, equity, and inclusion (DEI), and whether it gives back to communities. Note that the information below is designed to help you make better decisions as a shopper, employee, or member of a local community—not as an investor.

Vague promises don't lead to progress. Companies need to make measurable, time-bound commitments and performance goals. The first thing to note is whether the company has goals and provides sufficient information for you to evaluate their progress toward them.

The second thing to note is whether the company is tackling systemic issues or root causes of stubborn problems through partnerships and programs with other companies, nonprofits, or governmental organizations. One company acting alone can't solve big systemic issues such as slavery in agriculture, sweatshop labor, persistent pollution, waste in supply chains, breakthroughs in closed-loop production, or the transition to renewable energy in aviation or shipping. Look for a company's participation in partnerships, programs, and research to collaboratively address big issues.

Most of the information you need will appear in an annual sustainability report. Sometimes these reports are called environmental, social, and governance (ESG) reports, responsible business reports, corporate social responsibility (CSR) reports, impact reports, or integrated reports. Companies prepare these reports for many different audiences, so the formats and titles vary.

A Note on Regulation

Supply chain transparency has been largely increased because of consumer demand and reporting requirements. For example, the

2010 California Transparency in Supply Chains Act was the first such legislation that requires large companies operating within the state to disclose what, if anything, they are doing to ensure no slavery exists in their supply chains. The legislation was sourced by ASSET Campaign, an advocacy group working to ensure human rights in all supply chains, led by Julia Ormond, as a consumer information act. The same year, the U.S. Congress passed the Dodd-Frank Act, which included a reporting requirement on conflict minerals. Similar reporting regulations grew from these pioneering efforts and are now found in Australia, the European Union, the United Kingdom, and other countries. In 2024, European regulations increased the required transparency reporting on corporate accountability for labor and environmental conditions, as well as transparency about what goes into a product. This is good news for ratings and rankings companies that will use this additional data to score companies' efforts.

Find the Relevant Information

Go to the company's home page. If the words "sustainability," "environment," "social responsibility," "ESG," or "purpose" aren't on the home page, check the About tab. Alternatively use the search function to find the annual sustainability or ESG report. The landing page for the report may provide highlights, but most likely you'll want to look at the detailed report.

It's generally a bad sign if you can't easily find an annual sustainability report or information on sustainability, DEI, or purpose on the website. A company that strives to be a responsible business usually makes this information easy to locate.

Structure of Reports

You'll find many companies report with a set structure that covers their environmental and social policies and performance in addition to their governance. Each section addresses specific issues related to that category:

- Environmental: Covers the company's impact on the environment, such as greenhouse gas emissions, energy consumption, waste management, and water usage.
- Social: Focuses on the company's social impacts, including labor practices, community engagement, diversity and inclusion, and human rights.
- Governance: Examines the company's leadership, board composition, executive compensation, ethics, and compliance practices. Adherence to governing principles—such as the United Nations Guiding Principles on Human Rights and Global Compact—and membership in groups such as the World Council on Sustainable Development signal that the company's leadership considers global impacts on stakeholders and the environment.
- Data tables appear at the end of the report, along with details of the reporting standards used.

Planet Goals

Common environmental goals include greenhouse gas emission targets, uptake of renewable fuel, water use, and waste reduction. Look for targets that are specific and time bound, such as "reducing carbon emissions by 50 percent by 2030." This shows the company has a plan rather than just a vague intention.

The gold-standard goal for companies are Net Zero by 2050 or sooner, in alignment with the Science Based Targets Initiative

(SBTi)'s net zero standard. The Net Zero goal means the company must balance the amount of emitted greenhouse gases with an equivalent amount of reductions. The use of offsets or carbon credits is very limited, meaning a company must cut the amount of carbon it produces in real terms.

Alignment with SBTi targets assures that a company is making verifiable efforts—and not hollow promises—to reduce emissions in line with the need to keep the global temperature increase below 2°C (35.6°F) and pursuing efforts to limit warming to 1.5°C (34.7°F). The SBTi Net Zero standard is the most rigorous process for validating a company's climate change reduction efforts.

In addition to overall carbon reduction goals, look for commitments to increase the use of renewable energy. Is the company a part of the RE100, a group of hundreds of large and ambitious businesses committed to 100 percent renewable electricity? Renewable energy includes wind, geothermal, hydroelectric, biomass, new hydrogen technologies, and harnessing ocean tides' power. It's the quickest way for a company to reduce its greenhouse gas emissions.

For water, check for goals on reducing water usage, improving water quality, or investing in water-saving technologies. Water management is critical for the technology sector, as well as the food, beverage, and textile industries, including fashion.

Look for other environmental commitments as well, such as reducing waste, protecting biodiversity, or minimizing their overall environmental footprint. These sections of the report often include charts or graphs showing progress over time, giving you a sense of how long the company has been addressing environmental issues. I lean toward companies that have been improving their environmental footprint for many years.

People Goals

Look for details about labor practices, including in supply chains. Check the details about the company's supply chain practices: whether the company conducts regular third-party audits of its supply chain, and whether it publishes the results. Many companies have improvement goals, such as increasing the number of suppliers that are audited or certified for specific standards. Statements and goals on paying a living wage are strong indications of good practice.

I look for the certifications and standards mentioned in Chapter 7 and for business processes, such as SA8000 or ISO standards for factory and manufacturing practices. Most companies have codes of conduct for supply chains, but I always check to see whether the codes are audited and whether the company conducts assessments of its supply chain to identify and mitigate risks of labor abuse.

Labor abuse occurs for many reasons, many of which are linked to poverty and corruption. Check to see whether the company is participating in industry-led initiatives, partnerships, or programs with nonprofits to tackle the root issues of labor abuse, including education, factory training, and health services for workers.

For a large company, check whether it aligns with the United Nations Guiding Principles on Business and Human Rights. This isn't a program with specific goals. Rather, alignment indicates that the company understands its role in protecting the human rights of everyone impacted by the company.

A note on slavery: Today many companies are required by law to have a statement on their website about not engaging with slave labor. Companies often hide behind legally approved but action-deficient statements, such as "We do not tolerate the use of human trafficking, modern slavery or child labor in our operations or supply chain and encourage employees to take appropriate actions." This sounds good, but it provides no information about what the company is doing. Look for specifics, such as, "Assessing all suppliers and participating in annual third-party audits." How does it manage its work with suppliers in regions vulnerable to labor abuse? Does it review its codes of conduct with all suppliers?

Community Goals

Look for how the company supports and manages diverse communities internally through hiring and sourcing practices, as well as how it engages with local communities.

Diversity, equity, and inclusion (DEI) goals foster a more inclusive and equitable workplace. Goals often aim to increase the representation of underrepresented groups (based on gender, race, ethnicity, LGBTQ+ identification, people with disabilities, veterans) in the overall workforce by a specific percentage, especially in leadership roles. Look for goals for conducting pay equity audits to ensure that all employees are compensated fairly, regardless of their gender, race, or other demographic characteristics. Companies often have goals or report participation in training for leaders and managers on topics such as inclusive leadership, unconscious bias, and cultural competency.

Look to see whether a company partners with local suppliers and has goals for supplier diversity. For example, does a company have procurement policies that embrace local and minority-owned suppliers?

You can check how a company gives back to local communities and invests in local community projects, such as supporting community centers, parks, or educational facilities. Does the company sponsor local events, sports teams, or cultural activities? Does the company have an employee volunteer program so that employees can directly engage and give back?

Health Goals

For health-related issues, look for

- Certifications or third-party standards for nontoxic cosmetics, personal care, cleaning products, and clothing.
- Definition of any terms such as "clean," "natural," and "plant-based" that the company uses.
- Lists of ingredients allowed or not allowed in its products. For example, SC Johnson transparently explains how it screens ingredients through its Greenlist process. Many companies do not list or explain ingredients—a bad sign.
- Commitments with time frames to reformulate and remove specific toxic ingredients.
- Commitments to meet the highest standards globally on protecting health and the environment. European Union REACH regulations aim to protect human health and the environment from the risks of chemicals. REACH is tougher than most regulations in the United States and other countries. Does the global company apply REACH standards or better on products sold in the United States?

SUMMARY: GREEN LIGHT/RED LIGHT TABLES

The tables below summarize what to look for on a corporate website listed by environmental topics both in terms of positives (green lights) and negatives (red lights). Not all criteria apply to every company.

Table A1: Principles, Values, and Global Engagement in Company Reports

Principles, Values, and Global Engagement		
	Green Light	**Red Light**
Principles	Clearly stated commitment to sustainability, fair wages, human rights, and DEI	Vague values such as honesty, integrity, and respect with little or no detail about how they are defined and measured
Commitments	Commitment to United Nations Guiding Principles on Business and Human Rights, the Global Compact, membership in the World Business Council on Sustainable Development, or similar	No commitments

Table A2: People Issues in Company Reports

People		
	Green Light	**Red Light**
Slavery and Child Labor	Commitment to ending slavery, child labor, and abusive treatment of workers, with details about the company's efforts Certification and collaboration with organizations that support the most vulnerable people in supply chains (see Chapter 4)	Companies in industries with high risks of labor abuse (see Chapter 4) that offer no details on efforts to ensure fair and safe labor standards Vague or missing statement on slavery and child labor

Table A2: People Issues in Company Reports (Continued)

People		
	Green Light	**Red Light**
Fair Wages and Safe Working Conditions	Verification that its codes of conduct are followed by all suppliers Collaboration with organizations such as Fairtrade, Fair for Life, Nest, and others for workers' welfare and rights Participation in industry-led initiatives such as Better Cotton, or International Labor Organization (ILO) Better Factories Statements on paying a living wage, contracting only to factories that pay fair wages	No statement on wages, codes of conduct for suppliers, or benefits for workers in supply chains No mention of industry-led programs to improve working conditions in supply chains No partnerships or participation in programs for supply chain workers
Diversity, Equity, and Inclusion (DEI)	Data on employment by gender and underrepresented groups, preferably including specifics of employment at the director level and above Data on gender pay gaps Commitments to increase diversity at all levels of the company	Low or no diversity on board of directors No information about diversity in management or among executives No DEI goals

Table A3: Environmental Issues in Company Reports

Planet		
	Green Light	**Red Light**
Carbon Emissions	Commitments to either Net Zero or science-based targets by 2050 or earlier	No carbon emissions reporting No reduction goals, or weak goals, such as 30 percent reduction by 2050
Renewable Energy	Pledge Re 100	No plan for use of renewable energy Weak goals, such as 30 percent by 2030
Biodiversity and Deforestation	Time-bound commitments to zero deforestation As relevant by industry, commitments for • rainforest beef • no palm oil • FSC or other third-party certification for fish • pesticide pledge for pollinators Minimum effort: participation in industry groups such as Better Palm Oil Forest Stewardship Council or similar certifications Rainforest-free beef commitments Sustainable fishing commitments Commitment to support genetic diversity in crops	No reduction or mitigation goals for companies with palm oil, tropical timber, or other inputs or ingredients that drive deforestation Paper goods without sustainable forestry certification

Table A3: Environmental Issues in Company Reports (Continued)

Planet		
	Green Light	**Red Light**
Water Use and Pollution	A water strategy and time-bound commitments to: Reduce water usage intensity across all operations. Replenish more water than it consumes, especially in high water stress regions. Help provide access to water and sanitation services to people around the world. Share water-saving technologies with other companies.	No mention of water, especially for companies with large data centers, agricultural footprints, or textile manufacturing Companies in drought-prone areas with no water reduction goals
Waste: Single-Use Plastics	Commitments to get rid of all nonmedical single-use plastics, and/or to invest in new technology so that all packaging can be recycled by households by 2030	No mention of plastic wastes or commitment to reduce use of single-use plastics (for nonmedical applications)
Waste: Recyclables	Time-bound commitments to increase recyclable content and use recycled materials Time-bound commitment to increase the volume of material in closed-loop systems Member of the Ellen Mac-Arthur Foundation or similar efforts to increase the circular economy	Use of nonrecyclable materials with no commitment to change Products in excessive packaging and no commitment to innovate

Table A4: Health in Company Reports

Health		
	Green Light	**Red Light**
Nontoxic Ingredients	Certifications or third-party standards for nontoxic cleaning products List of ingredients allowed or not allowed	No certifications or clear statements about what is allowed or not allowed in products
Improvement Goals or Reformulation Goals	Commitments with time frames to reformulate and remove specific toxic ingredients; for example, removing all PFAS in athletic wear by 2030	No comment on reformulation or removing potentially toxic ingredients or ingredients banned in one country but allowed in others
Supply Chain	Goals to work with supply chain partners to ensure that harmful ingredients are not used in component parts	No mention of inputs and components

Table A5: Community Issues in Company Reports

Community		
	Green Light	**Red Light**
Diversity, Equity, and Inclusion (DEI)	Goals for an increase in the representation of underrepresented groups (e.g., attending to gender, race, ethnicity, LGBTQ+, people with disabilities, veterans) in the overall workforce, particularly in leadership roles	Vague statements about being an equal opportunity employer with no details or improvement goals
	Pay equity audits based on gender, race, or other demographic characteristics Hires neurodivergent staff Leadership training on inclusive leadership, unconscious bias, and cultural competency	No mention of training on DEI or a mechanism for advancement of underrepresented groups

Table A5: Community Issues in Company Reports (Continued)

Community		
	Green Light	**Red Light**
Local and Diverse Procurement Policies	Goals and strategies to increase procurement from local and diversely owned businesses for products and professional services	No mention of a procurement program
Community Giveback	Amounts donated in kind or in cash to local organizations Employee volunteer days in the community Skills and training for underrepresented groups or youth	Nonquantitative value statements about giving back and being a good neighbor No employee volunteer days

NOTES

1. Adella Shanahan, "Is Capital Consumption Allowance Included in GDP?," *TimesMojo* (blog), July 7, 2022, https://www.timesmojo.com/is-capital-consumption-allowance-included-in-gdp/.

2. For example, Julia Watkin, *Simply Living Well* (Boston: Houghton Mifflin Harcourt, 2020).

3. U.K. Foreign and Commonwealth Office, "The Rana Plaza Disaster," 2013, https://www.gov.uk/government/case-studies/the-rana-plaza-disaster.

4. Susan Weinschenk and Brian Wise, "Shopping, Dopamine, and Anticipation," *Psychology Today*, October 22, 2015, https://www.psychologytoday.com/us/blog/brain-wise/201510/shopping-dopamine-and-anticipation.

5. Jill Rosen, "Babies' Random Choices Become Their Preferences," Hub, October 2, 2020, https://hub.jhu.edu/2020/10/02/babies-prefer-what-they-choose-even-when-random/.

6. Solene Rauturier, "How Ethical Is Boohoo?," *Good On You* (blog), November 15, 2022, https://goodonyou.eco/how-ethical-is-boohoo/.

7. Archie Bland, Shah Meer Baloch, and Annie Kelly, "Boohoo Selling Clothes Made by Pakistani Workers 'Who Earned 29p an Hour.'" *The Guardian,* December 22, 2020, https://www.theguardian.com/business/2020/dec/22/boohoo-selling-clothes-made-by-pakistani-workers-who-earned-29p-an-hour.

8. Alex Assoune, "Boohoo," Panaprium, February 8, 2022, https://www.panaprium.com/blogs/i/boohoo.

9. Sustainalytics.com, "Company ESG Risk Rating—Sustainalytics," accessed August 29, 2024, https://www.sustainalytics.com /esg-rating.

10. Quartz, "Quartz Investigation: H&M Showed Bogus Environmental Scores for Its Clothing," June 29, 2022, https://qz.com/2180075/hm-showed-bogus-environmental-higg-index-scores-for-its-clothing.

11. Amanda Holpuch, "Twitter Bot Highlights Gender Pay Gap One Company at a Time," *New York Times,* March 9, 2022, https://www.nytimes.com/2022/03/09/business/pay-gap-international-womens-day-twitter.html.

12. Alice Chu and Osmud Rahman, "What Color Is Sustainable? Examining the Eco-Friendliness of Color," International Foundation of Fashion Technology Institutes Conference, Research Gate 2010, March 10, 2010, Taipei, Taiwan, https://www.researchgate.net/publication/332401739_What_color_is_sustainable_Examining_the_eco-friendliness_of_color.

13. Emily Brackett, "Color Theory: Blue as a Branding Color," *Branding Compass* (blog), December 27, 2019, https://brandingcompass.com/branding/color-theory-blue-as-a-branding-color/.

14. Will Bedingfield, "Why the Hell Can't McDonald's Recycle Its Paper Straws? It's Complicated," *Wired*, August 6, 2019, https://www.wired.com/story/mcdonalds-paper-plastic-straws-uk-recycling/.

15. Dieter Holger, "Coca-Cola Trials Turning Hard-to-Recycle Plastic into Bottles," *Wall Street Journal*, May 11, 2023, https://www.wsj.com/articles/coca-cola-trials-turning-hard-to-recycle-plastic-into-bottles-2f8d0dec.

16. Reuters, "Volkswagen Says Diesel Scandal Has Cost It 31.3 Billion Euros," March 17, 2020, https://www.reuters.com/article/us-volkswagen-results-diesel-idUSKBN2141JB/.

17. Irem Eren Erdogmus, Hadi Salari Lak, and Mesut Çiçek, "Attractive or Credible Celebrities: Who Endorses Green Products Better?," Procedia—*Social and Behavioral Sciences*, 12th International Strategic Management Conference, ISMC 2016, October 28–30, 2016, Antalya, Turkey, 235 (November 24, 2016): 587–94, https://doi.org/10.1016/j.sbspro.2016.11.085.

18. Jon Jacoby, "2 Million Children Laborers," e-mail to author, September 9, 2024.

19. Zachary Barlow, "Starbucks Hit with Greenwashing Suit," PracticalESG, January 16, 2024, https://practicalesg.com/2024/01/starbucks-hit-with-greenwashing-suit/.

20. Cocoa Life, "Cocoa Life—About the Program," accessed December 16, 2021, https://www.cocoalife.org/the-program/approach/.

21. Ibid.

22. U.S. Department of Labor, "Findings on the Worst Forms of Child Labor," September 2024, dol.gov/ChildLaborReports.

23. Julia Ormond, Phone interview with author, January 19, 2024.

24. U.N. Food and Agriculture Organization, "Tackling Climate Change Through Livestock: A Global Assessment of Emissions and Mitigation Opportunities," 2013, chrome-extension:/ /efaidnbmnnnibpcajpcglclefindmkaj/https://www.fao.org/3 /i3437e/i3437e.pdf.

25. Reporter Brazil, "Behind Starbucks Coffee," October 2023, chrome-extension://efaidnbmnnnibpcajpcglclefindmkaj /https://reporterbrasil.org.br/wp-content/uploads/2023/11 /monitor_starbucks_coffee_slave_labor_ENG.pdf.

26. Verónica Montúfar, "Women Are Most Likely to Be Affected by Violence in the Workplace, but We Are All Victims," *Public Services International* (blog), September 19, 2024, https:/ /publicservices.international/resources/news/women-are -most-likely-to-be-affected-by-violence-in-the-workplace -but-we-are-all-victims?id=6688&lang=en.

27. Allison Griffin, "Mexico's Garment Industry in 2019—Remake," April 22, 2019, https://remake.world/stories/news/mexicos -garment-industry-in-2019/.

28. Tugba Sabanoglu, "Leading Clothing Exporters Worldwide by Share 2022," Statista, July 2023, https://www .statista.com/statistics/1094515/share-of-the-leading-global -textile-clothing-by-country/.

29. The United Nations' standard for workers' rights includes freedom of association, elimination of all forms of forced or

compulsory labor, abolition of child labor, and elimination of discrimination in respect of employment and occupation. It does not cover wages.

30. In places where there is no minimum wage or where the minimum wage is considered too low to meet basic needs, a living wage can be estimated. A living wage is adjusted according to local living standards and is set through an analysis of the various basic expenses (food, clothing, housing, healthcare) that workers and their families face. Academics and workers' rights organizations estimate living wages for a range of cities around the world; however, many of the estimates are disputed for being below what an acceptable and dignified living standard requires.

31. Remake, "#PayHer: Amber Valletta, Nat Kelley on Inequities in Fashion," May 14, 2021, https://remake.world/stories/payherpercentE2percent80percent8B-amber-valletta-nat-kelley-on-inequities-in-fashion/.

32. International Brotherhood of Teamsters, "Overtime and Extended Work Shifts: Injuries, Illnesses, and Other Effects," August 3, 2016, https://teamster.org/overtime-and-extended-work-shifts-injuries-illnesses-and-other-effects/.

33. The lowest-wage countries are top of the list for low-complexity manufacturing, such as textiles, basic consumer goods, or simple mechanical devices like switches or circuit breakers.

34. Paul Barrett and Dorthee Bauman-Pauly, "Made in Ethiopia: Challenges in the Garment Industry's New Frontier by NYU Stern Center for Business and Human Rights—Issuu," May 3, 2019, https://issuu.com/nyusterncenterforbusinessandhumanri/docs/nyu_ethiopia_final_online.

35. Sarah Butler and Thaslima Begum, "Abuses 'Still Rife': 10 Years On from Bangladesh's Rana Plaza Disaster," *The Guardian,* April 24, 2023, https://www.theguardian.com/world/2023/apr/24/10 -years-on-bangladesh-rana-plaza-disaster-safety-garment -workers-rights-pay.

36. U.K. Foreign and Commonwealth Office, "The Rana Plaza Disaster," GOV.UK, 2013, https://www.gov.uk/government/case -studies/the-rana-plaza-disaster.

37. International Labor Office, United Nations Migration, and Walk Free, *Global Estimates of Modern Slavery: Forced Labor and Forced Marriage* (Geneva: International Labor Office, 2022), chrome -extension://efaidnbmnnnibpcajpcglclefindmkaj/https://www.ilo .org/sites/default/files/wcmsp5/groups/public/@ed_norm/ @ipec/documents/publication/wcms_854733.pdf.

38. UNICEF and International Labour Office, "Child Labour: Global Estimates 2020, Trends and the Road Forward," 2021, https:/ /www.unicef.org/protection/child-labour.

39. Know The Chain, "The Issue," accessed September 24, 2024, https://knowthechain.org/the-issue/.

40. Arriana McLymore, "Banned Chinese Cotton Found in 19 percent of US and Global Retailers' Merchandise, Study Shows," Reuters, May 7, 2024, https://www.reuters.com/markets /commodities/banned-chinese-cotton-found-19-us-retailers -merchandise-study-shows-2024-05-07/.

41. Jasmin Uddin, "Bangladesh's Apparel Export to USA Dips over 25 Percent in 2023," *Business Standard,* February 11, 2024, https:/ /www.tbsnews.net/economy/rmg/bangladeshs-apparel-export -usa-dips-over-25-2023-790774.

42. Transparentum, "Pandemic Pushes Struggling Tannery Workers to the Brink: Survey Shows Low Wages and Lack of Contracts Threaten the Livelihoods of Bangladeshi Tannery Workers," December 2020, https://www.transparentem.com.

43. Lykke E. Anderson, "Living Wage Update Report: Dhaka and Satellite Cities, Bangladesh," Living Wage Update Report, 2022, chrome-extension://efaidnbmnnnibpcajpcglclefindmkaj/https://www.globallivingwage.org/wp-content/uploads/2018/06/Updatereport_-Bangladesh-and-Satellite-Cities_-2022_30042022.pdf.

44. "In Bangladesh, Tanneries in Trouble," *Asia Foundation* (blog), May 27, 2020, https://asiafoundation.org/in-bangladesh-tanneries-in-trouble/.

45. Ibid.

46. Imtiaz Khan, "The Fascinating Tale of 'Made in Bangladesh' Leather," Osfelle, accessed September 24, 2024, https://osfelle.com/leather-industry-in-bangladesh/.

47. Fuzz Kitto, *Slavery as a Wicked Problem,* Slavery Unravelled, accessed November 6, 2024, https://www.beslaveryfree.com/podcast/slavery-as-a-wicked-problem.

48. Tony's Chocolonely, "Tony's Annual FAIR Reports," November 2022, https://tonyschocolonely.com/nl/en/annual-fair-reports/annual-fair-report-2021-2022.

49. Leonard Bonanni, "Forced Labor Is Embedded in Supply Chains. Here's How to Root It Out," Fast Company, June 16, 2021, https://www.fastcompany.com/906469/forced-labor-is-embedded-in-supply-chains-heres-how-to-root-it-out.

50. "Global Cosmetic Grade Mica Powder Market Research Report 2023," Market Intelligence Data, 2018, https://www.marketintelligencedata.com/reports/8516489/global-cosmetic-grade-mica-powder-market-research-report-2023?Mode=251sv.

51. World Vision, "Hidden Cost of Beauty: The Risk of Child Labour in Canadian Cosmetics," 2018, chrome-extension://efaid-nbmnnnibpcajpcglclefindmkaj/https://www.worldvision.ca/WorldVisionCanada/media/NCFS/Reports/risk-of-child-labour-in-canadian-cosmetics-mica-research-brief-2018.pdf.

52. U.S. Department of Labor, "List of Goods Produced by Child Labor or Forced Labor," September 2024, https://www.dol.gov/agencies/ilab/reports/child-labor/list-of-goods.

53. "Responsible Mica Initiative for a Responsible Mica," accessed April 25, 2022, https://responsible-mica-initiative.com/

54. Ronni Sandroff, "The History of Unions in the United States," Investopedia, March 12, 2024, https://www.investopedia.com/financial-edge/0113/the-history-of-unions-in-the-united-states.aspx.

55. Ruerd Ruben, "Why Do Coffee Farmers Stay Poor? Breaking Vicious Circles with Direct Payments from Profit Sharing," *Journal of Fair Trade* 4 (November 10, 2023).

56. Peter G. W. Keen, "From the Tea Fields: The Widening Labor vs. Machine Gap," STiR *Coffee and Tea Magazine,* August 17, 2021, https://stir-tea-coffee.com/api/content/0199e33e-ffd3-11eb-9a3a-1244d5f7c7c6/.

57. Food Empowerment Project, "Child Labor and Slavery in the Chocolate Industry," accessed September 24, 2024, https://food-ispower.org/human-labor-slavery/slavery-chocolate/.

58. Angie Aboa and Aaron Ross, "Child Labour Rising in West Africa Cocoa Farms Despite Efforts—Report," Reuters, October 19, 2020, https://www.reuters.com/article/world/child-labour-rising-in-west-africa-cocoa-farms-despite-efforts-report-idUSKBN2742GB/.

59. Seafood Watch, "Seafood Social Risk Tool," accessed January 29, 2024, https://www.seafoodwatch.org/our-projects/seafood-social-risk-tool.

60. Pay Up Fashion, "'H&M', Remake.word," April 12, 2022, https://remake.world/campaigns/.

61. Green America, "Chocolate Company Scorecard," March 28, 2023, https://www.greenamerica.org/chocolate-scorecard.

62. Emily Chan, "What Does the 'Made in' Label on Our Clothes Actually Mean?," *British Vogue*, January 18, 2024. https://www.vogue.co.uk/article/what-does-made-in-label-mean-clothes.

63. U.S. Department of State, "2023 Trafficking in Persons Report," June 2023, https://www.state.gov/reports/2023-trafficking-in-persons-report/.

64. Remake, "Remake Campaigns," April 12, 2022, https://remake.world/campaigns/.

65. Florian Schindler, "Water Efficiency in Textile Factories," Webinar, Berlin University of Applied Sciences and Technology, Berlin, Germany, September 19, 2023, chrome-extension://efaidnbmnnnibpcajpcglclefindmkaj/https://www.sia-toolbox.net/sites/default/files/2023-11/Trainingpercent20Programpercent20percent26percent20Curriculumpercent20Developmentpercent20onpercent20Sustainabilitypercent20inpercent20Textiles_8.2_Water_Efficiency.pdf.

66. Diana Ivanova, Konstantin Stadler, Kjartan Steen-Olsen, Richard Wood, Gibran Vita, Arnold Tukker, and Edgar G. Hertwich, "Environmental Impact Assessment of Household Consumption," *Journal of Industrial Ecology* 20, no. 3 (2016): 526–36, https://doi .org/10.1111/jiec.12371.

67. U.S. Environmental Protection Agency, Office of Air and Radiation, "Sources of Greenhouse Gas Emissions," Overviews and Factsheets, December 29, 2015, https://www.epa.gov /ghgemissions/sources-greenhouse-gas-emissions.

68. United Nations Development Programme, "What Do Plastics Have to Do with Climate Change?," November 15, 2022, https://stories.undp.org/what-do-plastics-have-to-do-with -climate-change.

69. U.N. Environment Programme, "Single-Use Plastics: A Roadmap for Sustainability," March 26, 2018, https://www.unep.org /resources/report/single-use-plastics-roadmap-sustainability.

70. United Nations Framework Convention on Climate Change, "The Paris Agreement," accessed March 7, 2024, https://unfccc .int/process-and-meetings/the-paris-agreement.

71. U.N. Food and Agriculture Association, "Tackling Climate Change Through Livestock: A Global Assessment of Emissions and Mitigation Opportunities," 2013, chrome-extension:/ /efaidnbmnnnibpcajpcglclefindmkaj/https://www.fao.org/3 /i3437e/i3437e.pdf.

72. McDonald's Corporation, "McDonald's Corporation Commitment on Forests," April 21, 2015, chrome-extension:/ /efaidnbmnnnibpcajpcglclefindmkaj/https://corporate .mcdonalds.com/content/dam/sites/corp/nfl/pdf /McDonaldsCommitmentOnForests.pdf.

73. U.N. Food and Agriculture Association, "COP26: Agricultural Expansion Drives Almost 90 Percent of Global Deforestation," March 10, 2024, https://www.fao.org /newsroom /detail/cop26-agricultural-expansion-drives-almost-90 -percent-of-global-deforestationen.

74. Yidi Xu, Le Yu, Philippe Ciais, Wei Li, Maurizio Santoro, Hui Yang, and Peng Gong, "Recent Expansion of Oil Palm Plantations into Carbon-Rich Forests," *Nature Sustainability* 5, no. 7 (July 2022): 574–77, https://doi.org/10.1038/s41893-022-00872-1.

75. Global Witness, "Products in US Supermarkets Linked to Deforestation of Tropical Forests," accessed September 1, 2024, https:/ /en/campaigns/forests/products-us-supermarkets-linked -deforestation-tropical-forests/.

76. World Wildlife Foundation, "Palm Oil Buyers Scorecards," accessed March 28, 2024, https://wwf.panda.org/discover /our_focus/food_practice/sustainable_production/palm_oil /scorecards/.

77. H. Purnomo, S. D. Kusumadewi, Q. P. Ilham, H. N. Kartikasara, B. Okarda, A. Dermawan, D. Puspitaloka, H. Kartodihardjo, R. Kharisma, and M. A. Brady, "Green Consumer Behaviour Influences Indonesian Palm Oil Sustainability," *International Forestry Review 25*, no. 4 (January 2024): 449–72, https://www.cifor-icraf .org/publications/pdf_files/articles/APurnomo2302.pdf.

78. Antonio Guterres, "Water Vital to Human Survival, Economic Development, Prosperity of Every Nation," United Nations, March 16, 2023, https://press.un.org/en/2023/sgsm21727.doc. htm.

79. National Integrated Drought Information System, "National Current Conditions," accessed November 21, 2024, https://www .drought.gov/current-conditions.

80. Columbia Water Center, "America's Water Stress Index," accessed June 19, 2024, https://water.columbia.edu/content/americas -water-stress-index.

81. Organisation of Economic Co-operation and Development, *How Green Is Household Behaviour? Sustainable Choices in a Time of Interlocking Crises,* OECD Studies on Environmental Policy and Household Behaviour, Paris, 2023, https://doi .org/10.1787/2bbbb663-en.

82. Raffaele Marfella, Francesco Prattichizzo, Celestino Sardu, et al., "Microplastics and Nanoplastics in Atheromas and Cardiovascular Events," *New England Journal of Medicine* 390, no. 10 (March 6, 2024): 900–910, https://www.nejm.org/doi /full/10.1056/NEJMoa2309822

83. Martin Pletz, "Ingested Microplastics: Do Humans Eat One Credit Card per Week?," *Journal of Hazardous Materials Letters* 3 (November 1, 2022): 100071, https://doi.org/10.1016/j .hazl.2022.100071.

84. National Institute of Standards and Technology, "Your Clothes Can Have an Afterlife," May 2022, https://www.nist.gov/news -events/news/2022/05/your-clothes-can-have-afterlife.

85. Shopify Plus, "Ecommerce Returns: Expert Guide to Best Practices (2024)," September 6, 2023, https://www.shopify.com /enterprise/blog/ecommerce-returns#0.

86. John Bartlett, "Chile's Atacama Desert Has Become a Fast Fashion Dumping Ground," *National Geographic,* March 5, 2024, https://www.nationalgeographic.com/environment/article /chile-fashion-pollution.

87. Tansy Hoskins and Karen Cass, *Foot Work: What Your Shoes Tell You About Globalisation,* (New York: Weidenfeld & Nicolson, 2020).

88. Tansy E. Hoskins, "'Some Soles Last 1,000 Years in Landfill': The Truth About the Sneaker Mountain," *The Guardian,* March 21, 2020, https://www.theguardian.com/fashion/2020/mar/21 /some-soles-last-1000-years-in-landfill-the-truth-about-the -sneaker-mountain.

89. Editors, "The Throwaway Generation: 25 Billion Styro-foam Cups a Year," *Emagazine.com* (blog), October 31, 2005, https://emagazine.com/the-throwaway-generation -25-billion-styrofoam-cups-a-year/.

90. U.S. Environmental Protection Agency and Office of Land and Emergency Management OLEM, "Containers and Packaging:Product-SpecificData,"September7,2017,https://www .epa.gov/facts-and-figures-about-materials-waste-and-recycling /containers-and-packaging-product-specific.

91. Cynthia Cummis, "This Is Leadership: Why Companies Are Set-ting Emissions Goals Based on Science," *Science Based Targets Initiative* (blog), May 20, 2015, https://sciencebasedtargets.org /blog/this-is-leadership-why-companies-are-setting-emissions -goals-based-on-science.

92. Unilever, "Unilever Rethinking-Plastic-Packaging," accessed March 28, 2024, https://www.unilever.com/planet-and-society/ waste-free-world/rethinking-plastic-packaging/.

93. American Cleaning Institute, "Cold Water Saves," accessed March 8, 2024, https://www.cleaninginstitute.org/industry-priorities /outreach/cold-water-saves.

94. Federal Reserve System, "Small Business Credit Survey: 2021 Report on Firms Owned by People of Color," 2021, chrome -extension://efaidnbmnnnibpcajpcglclefindmkaj/https://www .newyorkfed.org/medialibrary/FedSmallBusiness/files/2021 /sbcs-report-on-firms-owned-by-people-of-color.

95. Jason Wiens and Dane Stangler, "Snapshot: 7(a) Lending to Women-Owned Small Businesses," Bipartisan Policy Center, October 26, 2022, https://bipartisanpolicy.org/blog /snapshot-7a-women-owned-small-businesses/.

96. Timothy Carter, "The True Failure Rate of Small Businesses," *Entrepreneur,* January 3, 2021, https://www .entrepreneur.com/starting-a-business/the-true-failure-rate-of -small-businesses/361350.

97. Taylor Machette and Emily Boston, "Small Business, Big Impact: Small Retailers' Local Contributions," October 2023, https://www.cfib-fcei.ca/en/research-economic-analysis /small-retailers-local-contributions.

98. Stacy Mitchell, "Key Studies: Why Independent Matters," Institute for Local Self-Reliance, accessed June 25, 2024, https://ilsr .org/articles/key-studies-why-local-matters/.

99. Taylor Machette and Emily Boston, "Small Business, Big Impact: Small Retailers' Local Contributions," accessed June 25, 2024, https://www.cfib-fcei.ca/en/research-economic-analysis/small -retailers-local-contributions.

100. Jen Risley, "The Local Multiplier Effect," AMIBA, November 5, 2022, https://amiba.net/local-multiplier/.

101. Russel Redman, "Independent Supermarkets Drive One-Third of U.S. Grocery Sales," *Supermarket News,* June 15, 2021, https://www.supermarketnews.com/finance/independent -supermarkets-drive-one-third-of-u-s-grocery-sales.

102. Al Bondigas, "The Average Number of Patrons for a Coffee Shop," Bizfluent, June 15, 2021, https://bizfluent.com/the -average-number-of-patrons-for-a-coffee-shop.html.

103. Silvia Valencia, "Choosing a Restaurant Location," RestoHub, accessed April 10, 2024, https://www.touchbistro.com/blog /choosing-a-restaurant-location/.

104. Bill McKelvey, "Starting and Operating a Farmers Market: Frequently Asked Questions," University of Missouri Extension, May 2021, https://extension.missouri.edu/publications/g6223.

105. James Anthony, "74 Amazon Statistics You Must Know: 2023 Market Share Analysis & Data," financesonline.com, August 13, 2019, https://financesonline.com/amazon-statistics/.

106. Sarah Bradley, "How the Pandemic Changed Shopping Behavior," Think with Google, June 2021, https://www.thinkwith -google.com/consumer-insights/consumer-trends/pandemic -shopping-behavior/.

107. Ibid.

108. Ibid.

109. Wiens and Stangler, "Snapshot."

110. Rohit Arora, "Women-Owned Businesses Thrived in 2022," *Forbes,* accessed November 5, 2024, https://www

.forbes.com/sites/rohitarora/2023/03/08/women-owned
-businesses-thrived-in-2022/.

111. Ibid.

112. NerdWallet, "Small-Business Statistics: Numbers to Know
for 2023," May 11, 2023, https://www.nerdwallet.com/article
/small-business/small-business-statistics.

113. NerdWallet, "Black Business Owners Shut Out from Capital,"
January 8, 2021, https://www.nerdwallet.com/article/small
-business/racial-funding-gap.

114. Ibid.

115. Robert McFarlin IV, "Veterans Policy Is About More
Than the VA," *Forbes,* November 11, 2015, https://www
.forbes.com/sites/realspin/2015/11/11/veterans-policy
-is-about-more-than-the-va/.

116. The primary and universal definition of a refugee is contained
in the United Nations 1951 Refugee Convention, which es-
tablishes the conditions under which a person becomes a refugee. Refugees are afforded international protection by other
countries because it is too dangerous for the refugees to return
home. An asylum seeker is someone whose request for sanc-
tuary has yet to be processed. Once asylum seekers are recognized as refugees, they can receive legal and material assistance
from the host country government.

117. National Immigration Forum, "Immigrants as Economic
Contributors: Refugees Are a Fiscal Success Story for
America," June 14, 2018, https://immigrationforum.org/article
/immigrants-as-economic-contributors-refugees-are-a
-fiscal-success-story-for-america/.

118. Katie Auchenbach, "Small Business Ownership by People with Disabilities: Challenges and Opportunities," *National Disability Institute* (blog), July 25, 2022, https://www.nationaldisabilityinstitute.org/reports/small-business-ownership-pwd-challenges-and-opportunities/.

119. J. P. Morgan, "The Benefits & Steps to LGBTQ+ Business Certification," January 24, 2023, https://www.jpmorgan.com/insights/corporate-responsibility/diversity-equity-and-inclusion/the-benefits-and-steps-to-lgbt-business-certification.

120. Dan Clark, "How Many U.S. Adults Have a Criminal Record?," @politifact. accessed November 5, 2024, https://www.politifact.com/factchecks/2017/aug/18/andrew-cuomo/yes-one-three-us-adults-have-criminal-record/.

121. Amy Soloman, "In Search of a Job: Criminal Records as Barriers to Employment," National Institute of Justice, June 14, 2012, https://nij.ojp.gov/topics/articles/search-job-criminal-records-barriers-employment.

122. Alonzo Martinez, "From Open Hiring to Negligent Hiring: How to Reduce Risk and Promote Inclusivity," *Forbes,* February 24, 2020, https://www.forbes.com/sites/alonzomartinez/2020/02/24/from-open-hiring-to-negligent-hiring-how-to-reduce-risk-and-promote-inclusivity/.

123. Seth Godin, "But It Matters a Lot to Them . . . ," *Seth's Blog,* October 2, 2023, https://p.feedblitz.com/r3.asp?l=231309227&f=1081591&c=13427588&u=22772416.

124. Sarah Kobylewski and Michael F. Jacobson, "Toxicology of Food Dyes," *International Journal of Occupational and Environmental Health* 18, no. 3 (2012): 220–46, https://doi.org/10.1179/1077352512Z.00000000034.

125. Bruna Fernandes Azevedo, Lorena Barros Furieri, Franck Maciel Peçanha, et al., "Toxic Effects of Mercury on the Cardiovascular and Central Nervous Systems," *Journal of Biomedicine and Biotechnology* (2012): 949048, https://doi.org/10.1155/2012/949048.

126. Harvard Health, "What to Do About Mercury in Fish," July 28, 2017, https://www.health.harvard.edu/staying-healthy/what-to-do-about-mercury-in-fish.

127. Center for Food Safety and Applied Nutrition, "Mercury Levels in Commercial Fish and Shellfish (1990–2012)," U.S. Food and Drug Administration, December 21, 2023, https://www.fda.gov/food/environmental-contaminants-food/mercury-levels-commercial-fish-and-shellfish-1990-2012.

128. Emily Main and Rachel Clark, "12 Fish You Should Never Eat (and What to Eat Instead)," *Good Housekeeping,* November 29, 2021, https://www.goodhousekeeping.com/health/diet-nutrition/a20705842/fish-you-should-never-eat/.

129. U.S. Environmental Protection Agency, Office of Water, "EPA-FDA Advice About Eating Fish and Shellfish," July 30, 2015, https://www.epa.gov/choose-fish-and-shellfish-wisely/epa-fda-advice-about-eating-fish-and-shellfish.

130. Emily Main and Rachel Clark, "12 Fish You Should Never Eat (and What to Eat Instead)," *Good Housekeeping,* November 29, 2021, https://www.goodhousekeeping.com/health/diet-nutrition/a20705842/fish-you-should-never-eat/.

131. Center for Food Safety and Applied Nutrition, "Mercury Levels in Commercial Fish and Shellfish (1990–2012)," U.S. Food and Drug Administration, December 21, 2023, https:/ /www.fda.gov/food/environmental-contaminants-food /mercury-levels-commercial-fish-and-shellfish-1990-2012.

132. U.S. Department of State, "2023 Trafficking in Persons Report," June 2024, https://www.state.gov/reports/2023 -trafficking-in-persons-report/.

133. Environmental Justice Foundation, "Illegal Fishing and Human Rights Abuse in China's Distant Water Fleet," April 2022, https://ejfoundation.org/news-media/global-impact-of -illegal-fishing-and-human-rights-abuse-in-chinas-vast -distant-water-fleet-revealed-2.

134. Margie Mason, Robin McDowell, Martha Mendoza, and Ester Htusun, "Global Supermarkets Selling Shrimp Peeled by Slaves," Associated Press, December 14, 2015, http://www .ap.org/explore/seafood-from-slaves/global-supermarkets -selling-shrimp-peeled-by-slaves.html.

135. EWG, "About Skin Deep® Cosmetics Database," accessed February 1, 2024, http://www.ewg.org/skindeep/learn_more/about/.

136. EWG, "EWG's Pledge to Protect Your Health—Our Mission," September 30, 2020, https://www.ewg.org/who-we-are /our-mission.

137. Campaign for Safe Cosmetics, "Making Cosmetics Safer for All," accessed January 26, 2024, https://www.safecosmetics.org/.

138. Romy Fraser, "Clean Cosmetics Work," e-mail to author, September 6, 2024.

139. Environmental Working Group, "Spring Clean Your Cosmetics: Go Without These 6 Ingredients," April 2, 2010, https://www.ewg.org/news-insights/news/spring-clean-your-cosmetics-go-without-these-6-ingredients.

140. Susan Curtis and Romy Fraser, *Natural Healing for Women: Caring for Yourself with Herbs, Homeopathy & Essential Oils.* Thorsons Publishers Limited, (London: 1992).

141. Ebru Karpuzoglu, Steven D. Holladay, and Robert M. Gogal Jr., "Parabens: Potential Impact of Low-Affinity Estrogen Receptor Binding Chemicals on Human Health," *Journal of Toxicology and Environmental Health, Part B* 16, no. 5 (July 4, 2013): 321–35, https://doi.org/10.1080/10937404.2013.809252.

142. Scientific Committee on Consumer Safety, "Opinion on Quaternium-15 (Cis-Isomer)," European Commission: Directorate General Health and Consumers, December 13, 2011, chrome-extension://efaidnbmnnnibpcajpcglclefindmkaj/https://ec.europa.eu/health/scientific_committees/consumer_safety/docs/sccs_o_077.pdf.

143. Environmental Working Group, "Cancer-Causing Chemical 1,4-Dioxane Contaminates Americans' Drinking Water," September 6, 2017, https://www.ewg.org/news-insights/news/cancer-causing-chemical-14-dioxane-contaminates-americans-drinking-water.

144. U.S. Environmental Protection Agency, Office of Chemical Safety and Pollution Prevention, "Identifying Greener Cleaning Products," November 20, 2014, https://www.epa.gov/greenerproducts/identifying-greener-cleaning-products.

145. Alden Wicker, *To Dye For,* (New York: G.P. Putnam's Sons, 2023).

146. Ibid.

147. Ibid.

148. Lena Milton, "How To Make Sure Your Clothes Are Non-toxic (To You and the Environment!)," A Sustainable Closet, accessed September 9, 2024, https://www.asustainablecloset.com/home /how-to-make-sure-your-clothes-are-non-toxic-to-you-and -the-environment.

149. Sonderlier, "The Hidden Chemicals in Your Clothes, and How to Detox Your Wardrobe," July 21, 2023, https://sonderlier .com/blogs/journal/shop-clean-dress-nontoxic.

150. Molly Wanner and Neera Nathan, "Clean Cosmetics: The Science Behind the Trend," Harvard Health, March 4, 2019, https://www.health.harvard.edu/blog/clean-cosmetics-the -science-behind-the-trend-2019030416066.

151. Leon Pieter, Daniel Pankratz, David Novak, and Stephen Rogers, "The Cost of Buying Green," Deloitte Insights, June 17, 2022, https://www2.deloitte.com/us/en/insights/industry /retail-distribution/consumer-behavior-trends-state-of-the -consumer-tracker/sustainable-products-and-practices-for -green-living.html.

152. Investors Report, "J Crew ESG Report 2023," accessed August 29, 2024, chrome-extension://efaidnbmnnnibpcajpcglclefindmkaj /https://investors.jcrew.com/static-files /9786d180-2a54-40df -9d6a-c13d733f7362.

153. For example, Julia Watkin, *Simply Living Well,* (Boston and New York: Houghton Mifflin Harcourt, 2020).

154. Amy Brown,"Resale Is All the Rage, but Fashion Brands Not Making a Dent in Unsustainable Levels of Waste," Reuters, August 9, 2023, https://www.reuters.com/sustainability/climate -energy/resale-is-all-rage-fashion-brands-not-making-dent -unsustainable-levels-waste-2023-08-09/.

155. Alex Assoune, "The Small Number of Times the Average Piece of Clothing Is Worn," Panaprium, March 26, 2020, https:/ /www.panaprium.com/blogs/i/times-clothing-worn.

PERMISSIONS

The following companies have granted permission to use logos and graphics:

A Greener World

B Lab

Bluesign Technologies AG

Cradle to Cradle Products Innovation Institute

Disability:IN

Environmental Working Group

Equal Exchange

Fair Trade USA

Fibershed

Forest Stewardship Council

Gender Fair

Global Organic Textile Standard

GoodWeave International

International Natural and Organic Cosmetics Association

Land to Market

MADE SAFE

Marine Stewardship Council

Nest

NSF

OEKO-TEX

Positive Luxury

Quality Assurance International (QAI)

Rainforest Alliance

Regenerative Organic Alliance

Slow Food USA

Sustainable Forest Initiative

UL Solutions

U.S. Black Chambers, Inc.

U.S. Cotton Trust Protocal

U.S. Environmental Protection Agency ENERGY STAR
Labeled Products Program and Safer Choices Program

USDA Organic

Veteran Owned Businesses

Women's Business Enterprise National Council

World Fair Trade Organization

INDEX

A

ACA. *See* American Cosmetic Association
Adidas, 95
African American Chamber of Commerce, 133
agents for brands, 46
A Greener World, 106–7
agriculture
    driving biodiversity loss, 82
    regenerative, 94
    air fresheners, 189
Allbirds, 66, 108
Alter Eco, 71
Amazon, 122, 140, 141, 185, 203, 211, 221
    minority-owned storefronts, 133
    women-owned business storefront, 131
Amazon's Climate Pledge Friendly listings, 102, 111
American Cosmetic Association, 177, 179
American Indian Food Market, 221

American Indian Foods website, 134
Amfori, 69
Animals Raised without Antibiotics, 174
animal testing, 162
antibacterial hand soap, 189
Ark of Taste, 109
Arm & Hammer, 93
Armani, 54
Arts and Crafts Board Directory, 139
Athleta, 66, 108
at-home work, 65
azo dyes, 167

B

Badoit, 214
bananas
    plantations for, 60
    varieties of, 83
Bangladesh
    child labor in, 53–54
    fast-fashion production in, 48–49
Bass, 54
BBE (best before) dates, 163

B Corps, 12, 66–67, 93, 108, 222
Beaumont Organic, 183
bees, 82–83, 99
beet sugar, 60
Ben & Jerry's, 66, 108, 128
Better Buying, 47
Better Cotton Initiative, 68
Better Factories Initiative, 68
Better Factories program (ILO), 35
Better Sugar Initiative, 68
Better Work, 69
Beyond Buckskin, 140
bicycle repair centers, 211
biodiversity, 93
    as Earth system, 81–85
    high-impact switches for, 114–15
    loss of, 80, 98–99
    measuring companies' impact on, 92
biomass, 94
Bisphenol A (BPA), 167
B Labs, 66, 108
Black Business Green Book, 139
Black Friday, 13
Black and Green, 221
bleaches, 189
bloggers, 136, 141
bluesign, 183–84
bluesign APPROVED, 184
bluesign certified, 172
bluesign PRODUCT, 184
bluewashing, 24–26, 32
Bombas, 66, 108
Bonsucro, 60
Boohoo, 23–24
borrowing, 10, 204
BPA. See Bisphenol A
brands
    consumers communicating with,
        74–75, 113–14, 142–43, 190–91
    mapping their supply chains, 47
    pricing and, 197
    purchasing practices of, 46
Branson, Richard, 128

Brazil
    cattle production in, 84
    mica mining in, 56
    slaves in, 72
brominated vegetable oil, 149
businesses, certifications for, 131–35
Business Insider, 98
Butterfly Mark, 32, 34, 65–66
Buycott, 71
buyer's remorse, 14
buying local, 9, 119–22. See also
    locally owned businesses
buying secondhand, 204
Buy Nothing Project, 211
Buy Women Owned, 136, 139
ByBlack Platform, 133
bycatch, 83–84
By Rotation, 209

C

C.A.F.E. standards (coffee), 33, 34, 38
California Environmental Protection
    Agency, Office of Environmental
    Health, 149–50
Calvin Klein, 70
Campaign for Safe Cosmetics, 158,
    180, 221
Carbon Almanac, 19
carbon emissions, 81–82
carbon reduction goals, 91–92
Cargil, 71
cattle production, 84
Cavendish bananas, 83
C Corporation, 108
celebrity-washing, 29–30, 140
Centers for Disease Control and
    Prevention, 171
Central Africa
    deforestation in, 85
    slavery and child labor in, 51
Central America, deforestation in, 85
Central Market, 130
Central Mexico, butterflies and, 84
certification bodies, 32

certification marks, 31–36
certification programs, 24, 31–36,
    45–46, 62–69
Certified American Humane
    (USDA), 173
certified fair labor products, 219
Certified Humane (USDA), 173
Certified Plant Based, 174
certified products, 35–36
certified sustainable companies.
    See B Corps
Chambers of Commerce, 137, 143
Chanel No. 5, 157
Change the World by How You Shop,
    139
checkfresh.com, 163
chemical exposure, flow of, 165
chemical waste, 90
child labor, 30-32, 49–50, 53–54
China
    mica mining in, 56
    slavery and forced and child
        labor in, 50-51
    tuna from, 61
chlorine bleach, 171
chocolate
    child labor and, 59–60
    ratings for, 70
Chocolate Score Card, 58, 70–71,
    109, 221
circular business models, 106, 212–14
Clean Fifteen (EWG), 151–52, 204,
    221
Clearya, 186, 203
climate
    as Earth system, 80–81
    high-impact switches for, 114
Climate Beneficial, 107–8
climate change, 81, 82, 98
closed-loop models, 80, 93, 207,
    212–14
cloth, certified organic, 168

clothing
    avoiding health hazards with,
        171–72
    certifications for, 182–84
    closed-loop systems for, 213–14
    cost of buying locally, 200
    high-impact switches for, 193
    length of time worn, 215–16
    manufacturing of, 5
    rental of, 209–10
    treated with chemicals, 166–68
    unwanted, treatment of, 88–89
Cluey Consumer, 109
Coach, 54
Coca-Cola, 27, 214
Cocoa Life, 34
coconut water, 94
coffee, switching buying habits for, 59
colors, listed on nutrition labels, 153
Columbia Water Center, 86
commercial buildings, 100
communities
    connecting with, 15–16
    economic support of, 220
companies, environmental
    impact of, 91–95
company-designed marks, 33–35
company websites, evaluating, 28
compromises, 20
Connected Butterfly Mark
    Digital Brand Passport, 66
Conscious Customer, 110
Conservation International, 33
"Contains Organic Ingredients," 175
Cornshucker, Mel, 16
Cos, 99
CosmEthics, 187
cosmetics, 157–64
    apps and databases for, 185–87
    avoiding health hazards with,
        170–71
    certification programs for, 174–79
    high-impact switches for, 192
    shelf life of, 162–64

Cosmily, 187
COSMOS, 103
COSMOS NATURAL, 103, 176
COSMOS ORGANIC, 103, 176
Costco, 35, 101
cost-conscious shopping, tips on,
    202–5
Cotopaxi, 63
cotton, 67, 79–80
coupon apps, 138
Cradle to Cradle Certified, 106
criminal backgrounds, hiring people
    with, 128
Cruelty Free, 177
Cruelty-Free Shopping Guide
    (PETA), 177
CSC. *See* Campaign for Safe
Cosmetics
C2C. *See* Cradle to Cradle Certified
Curtis, Susan, 160

D
Danone, 92
DBP. *See* dibutyl phthalate
deceptive marketing, 25–28
deforestation, 80, 82, 84–86, 103
high-impact switches for, 114–15
shopping decisions and, 98
DEI. *See* diversity, equity, and
    inclusion
denim, water used in production of, 87
DeTox Me, 186
diazolidinyl urea (Germall II), 161
dibutyl phthalate, 161
Dior Couture, 33
direct-from-farm options, 207, 215
Dirty Dozen (EWG), 151–52, 170,
    204, 221
Disability Owned Business
    Enterprise, 134–35
disinfectant wipes, 171, 190, 193
disposable packaging, 90
disposable plastics, 96
diversity, equity, and inclusion, 57

DMDM hydantoin (Glydant), 161
DOBE. *See* Disability Owned
    Business Enterprise
Dole, 35
dolphins, caught in fishing nets, 3–4
DoneGood, 71
dopamine, 13–14
drain cleaners, 190, 193
Dr. Bronner's Soap, 63
Dr. Hauschka, 56, 178
dry cleaning, 190
due diligence processes, 54–55
Dyson, 211

E
Earth, interrelated biophysical
    processes of, 80–81
EatOkra, 139
EatWellGuide.org, 138
Ecocert, 102–3
Eco Cult, 188, 221
Ecosystem Approach (MADE SAFE),
    180
Ecuador, tuna from, 61
Eileen Fisher, 63, 203, 211, 214
Ellen MacArthur Foundation, 216
employees, companies' treatment of,
    8, 11–12
endocrine disruptors, 160–61, 168,
    174
ENERGY STAR, 32, 36, 100, 221
energy use, shopping decisions and,
    98
environmental certifications, 49,
    99–108
environmental damage, stopping, 3
environmental impact
    avoiding the worst offenders in,
        111–12
    databases and directories for,
        109–11
    rating systems for, 109–11
environmentally friendly purchasing,
    219

environmentally responsible products, 8
Environmental Protection Agency, 89
Environmental Working Group, 158, 160, 170, 185, 221
EPA Safer Choice, 181
equal employment opportunities, 126–27
Equal Exchange, 59, 68
Estée Lauder, 56
ethical and sustainable goods, cost of, 10, 196–202
Ethical Consumer, 69, 72
Ethical Handcraft program, 65
Ethiopia, wages in, 48
Etsy, 137, 140, 141, 203, 221
Europe
cracking down on greenwashing, 28
information disclosure in, 47
European Union, deforestation regulations in, 85, 92
Everlane, 94
Evian, 214
EWG. *See* Environmental Working Group
EWG Verified, 174–75, 180, 221
EWG Verified: For Your Health, 188
exfoliation, 162
eye cosmetics, 164

F
Facebook, 142
Facebook groups, 137
Facebook Marketplace, 211
fair labor certifications, 49
Fair Labor Organization, 69
Fair for Life, 33, 38, 59, 63, 76–77, 234
Fair Trade, 59, 62–63
Fair Trade Certified, 4, 6, 10, 33, 38, 62–63, 203, 221
fair trade ingredients, 63
Fairtrade International, 62–63
Fair Trade USA certification, 32–33, 36, 49

fair trade wages, 15
fake certification logos, 99–100
false narratives. *See* storytelling
Farmers Market Directory (USDA), 138
farmers' markets, 117–18, 121, 138, 173
farm-to-textile options, 99
fashion
carbon emissions and, 98
ratings for, 69–70
Fashion Accountability Report (Remake), 69
fast fashion, 48–49, 203–4
Fat Llama, 208
FDA certifications, for cosmetics, 175
Federal Bureau of Investigation, 128
Federal Trade Commission, 166
female empowerment, 25
Ferrara, 60
Fibershed, 107–8
fish
country of origin, 61
higher-risk, 155–56
mercury poisoning and, 153–56
sustainable, 112
Fish Advisories and Safe Eating Guidelines (EPA), 155
fishing, labor abuses and, 60–61
5-R Rule, 6
food
avoiding health hazards with, 170
certifications for, 172–74
cost of buying locally, 199–200
high-impact switches for, 192
imported into the U.S., 172–73
rating systems, directories, and apps for, 185
sourcing well, 204–5
toxic chemicals and coloring in, 148–52
FoodData Central (USDA), 185
food dyes, 152-153

Food Scores (EWG), 185
forced labor, 49–50. *See also* child
    labor; slavery
Forest Stewardship Council, 103–4,
    201, 221
forever chemicals, 90, 166, 167
formaldehyde, 168
formaldehyde releasers, 161
4 Objects, 93, 211
fragrances, secret formulas for, 157,
    160
France, circularity in, 214
Fraser, Romy, 159–60
free range, 173
frequent purchases, high-impact
    switches for, 76–77, 95–97,
114–15, 144–45
Frida Pickles, 127
FSC. *See* Forest Stewardship Council
FSC 100®, 103
FSC Mix®, 104
FSC Recycled®, 103

G
Gain, 93
garment production, supply chain
    for, 44–45
garment workers' rights, 70
Gayborhood, 140
gender equality, 57
gender equity, 132
Gender Fair, 132, 221
General Mills, 86
generosity, acts of, 15
GettinLocal, 138
Girlfriend Collective, 183
Global Organic Textile Standard
(GOTS), 102–3, 182, 221
Gluten Free, 174
Godin, Seth, 144
Godiva chocolate, 58
Good On You, 70, 71, 110, 203
GoodWeave, 32–33, 36, 64–65
GoodWeave International, 31–32

Google, 137, 142
GOTS. *See* Global Organic Textile
    Standard
GOTS certified, 172
GRAS (generally recognized as safe),
    179
gratitude, 16, 21
Grayston Bakery, 128–29
Green Frog certification, 35, 49, 64
greenhouse gases, 81, 87–88, 92
Green Seal, 101–2, 221
Green 3, 153
greenwashing, 7, 100, 23–30, 32
Groupon, 138
Gucci, 30, 44
Guide to Healthy Cleaning (EWG),
    180
guilt, assuaging of, 17–18
H
habits, formation of, 17, 218–19
handcrafted items, demand for,
    45–46
Hanna Andersson, 183
Hannaford, 130
happiness, 14–15, 16, 21
health hazards, shopping to avoid,
    147–48
Healthy Living (EWG), 188
healthy products, switching to, 220
Heard Indian Fair and Market
    (Phoenix), 16
H.E.B., 130
Heinen's, 130
Herman Miller, 95
Hershey, 60
high-risk countries, avoiding
    products from, 72–74
H&M, 25, 213, 216
home appliances, 100
household cleaning products, 164–66
    apps and databases for, 188
    avoiding, 171, 189–90
    certifications for, 179–82

high-impact switches for, 192–93
homemade, 205
Hugo Boss, 54
Hush Puppies, 54
hydroxy acids, 162
Hy-ve, 130

I

IAC. *See* Intertribal Agriculture
  Council
IKEA, 211
ILO. *See* International Labour
  Organization
imidazolidinyl urea (Germall 115), 161
INCI Beauty, 187
INCIDecoder, 187
India
  mica mining in, 56
  shrimp farming in, 61
Indian Arts and Crafts Board, 139
Indigenous Artisan Collective, 140
Indonesia, deforestation in, 85, 86
industrial plants, 100
industry collaborations, 68–69
influencers, 140
infrequent purchases, high-impact
  switches for, 77, 114–15, 145–46,
    192–93
intentional shopping, 17–18
International Accord for Health and
  Safety in the Textile and Garment
  Industry, 49
International Labor Office, 61
International Labour Organization,
  35
International Nomenclature
  Cosmetic Ingredient systems, 187
International Women's Day, 25
Intertribal Agriculture Council, 133
invasive species, 82
Irish potato famine (1845), 83

J

Jacoby, Jon, 31–32
J. Crew Group, 4, 203

K

Kardashian, Kourtney, 23, 24
Kazakhstan, forced child labor in, 72
Kellogg's, 86
Kering, 30
Kickstand, 211
Kiehl's, 33, 34
kindness, acts of, 15
Kroger, 99

L

labor, abusive practices and, 3, 42-43
labor unions, 57
landfills, 87
land management
  high-impact switches for, 114–15
  shopping decisions and, 98–99
Land to Market, 102
land use, as Earth system, 81, 85–86
laundry detergent, 93
laureth, 161
LeafScore, 71
Leaping Bunny, 32–33, 162, 177, 186
leather, alternatives to, 94
leather industry, child labor in, 53–54
Leather Working Group, 35
Levi Strauss & Co. (Levi's), 3, 44, 67,
  87, 211
LGBTQ+ businesses, 126
LGBTQ+ nondiscrimination, 57
lifestyle goods, ratings for, 71–72
lifetime value, 198–99
lipstick, 169
Living Social, 138
living wage, 47
Local Flavor, 138
LocalHarvest.org, 138
locally owned businesses, 118–22,
  142–43
local produce, in grocery stores, 130
L'Oreal, 15, 56
Lorina, 214
low-wage countries, moving work
  to, 48

M

Macy's, 65
Madagascar, mica mining in, 56
Madewell brands, 4, 63, 65, 203
Made51.org, 68
"made in" labels, 11, 54, 72
MADE SAFE, 180
Malaysia, deforestation in, 85
maquilas, 42
Marine Stewardship Council, 98–99,
    105, 112, 221
Marriott, 127
Mars, 60
MBE. *See* Minority Business Enterprise
McDonald's, 27, 84–85
Meiji, 60
mercury poisoning, 153–56
methane, 87–88
Mexico
maquilas in, 42
monarch butterflies' arrival in, 84
    slaves in, 72
mica, 50, 55–56, 219
Michelin, 15
microplastics, 88
military spouses, 125
Minority Business Enterprise,
    132–33, 143
minority-owned businesses, 9,
    118–19, 122, 123–24
Modern Meadows, 94
monarch butterfly, migration of, 84
Mondelēz International, 34, 60, 86
Monterey Bay Aquarium, 112
Moth, David, 127
MSC. *See* Marine Stewardship
    Council
MycoWorks, 94

N

National Gay and Lesbian Chamber
    of Commerce, 126
National LGBT Chamber of
    Commerce, 135

Nativa, 99, 215
Native American Made Products,
    133–34
Native American tribal certifications,
    133
Natrue (International Natural and
    Organic Cosmetics Association),
    178
natural fibers, 168
natural food coloring, 152–53
natural fragrances, 160
Natural Products Association,
    178–79, 182
natural resources, all products
    originating from, 79–80
NatureHub, 110
Nest, 36, 45–46, 65
Nestlé, 38, 60, 71, 86, 92
neurodiverse hiring, 126–28
new materials, 94–95
news media, as source for company
    information, 29
New York Times, investigation on U.S.
    child labor, 52, 55
Nextdoor, 137–38, 211
NGLCC. *See* National LGBT
    Chamber of Commerce
Nirapon, 69
nitrosamine, 161
Non-GMO, 174
Non-Toxic Black Beauty Project
    (CSC), 186
North American beet sugar, 60
North Face, 211, 213
NPA. *See* Natural Products
    Association
NSF, 175–76
NSF/ANSI 305, 175–76
Nudie Jeans, 211
Nully, 209

O

OCS (Organic Content Standard),
    103

Odylique, 56
OEKO-TEX certified, 172
OEKO-TEX Made in Green, 183
OEKO-TEX Standard 100, 183
OEKO-TEX Standards, 183
   1,4-dioxane, 161
   "100 percent organic," 150
   "100 Percent Organic" (USDA),
      173
online information
   directories, 137
   platforms, 137
   ratings, 136
   reviews, 142
   trustworthiness of, 135–36
online shopping
   dopamine and, 13
   platforms for, 140
online tools, types of, 137
Open Arms Studio, 125
open-door hiring policy, 128–29
"organic," 151
organic certified, 172
organic clothing, 168
organic cosmetics, 159
organic foods, 101, 150
"organic ingredients listed," 151
"organic [name of ingredient]," 151
organic products, certification of,
   150–51
Ormond, Julia, 37
oven cleaners, 190
overfishing, 82, 83–84

P

packaging, 89, 92
packaging waste, 90, 97, 122
Pakistan
   mica mining in, 56
   worker reforms in, 49
palm oil, 80, 85–86, 97
Palm Oil Scan, 110
Palm Oil Score Card, 110
PAO (period after opening), 163

paper products, 98
paper straws, 27
parabens, 160
Parley for the Oceans, 95
Patagonia, 34, 63, 65, 66, 108, 211, 213
Paula's Choice Skin Care Ingredient
   Checker, 187
Paycheck Protection Program (PPP)
   loans, 124
pay equity, 25, 57
#PayUp campaign, 70
peer-to-peer rentals, 208–9
peers, buying from, 10
PEG. *See* polyethylene glycol
people with disabilities
   businesses owned by, 124, 126
c ompanies hiring, 127
People for the Ethical Treatment of
   Animals, 177, 186
perfection, quandary of, 37–39
perfectionism, 24
perfluoroalkyl and polyfluoroalkyl
   substances, 90–91, 166, 167
Persil, 93
Personal Care certification (NPA), 182
personal care products, 157–64
avoiding health hazards with, 170–71
high-impact switches for, 192
Personal Care Products Council, 157
Peru, mica mining in, 56
pesticides, 83, 149
PET. *See* polyethylene terephthalate
   plastic
PETA. *See* People for the Ethical
   Treatment of Animals
PFAS. *See* perfluoroalkyl and
   polyfluoroalkyl substances
PFAS Central, 110
PFCs, 167
PFOAs, 167
phthalates, 161, 168
Picard, 54
Pickle, 209
Pink Spot, 140

plant genetic diversity, 83
plastics, 96
    exposure to, 88
    greenhouse gases and, 81
    unrecyclable, 90
pollinators, 82–83, 99
pollution, 82
polyethylene, 161
polyethylene glycol, 161
polyethylene terephthalate plastic, 92
positive behaviors, signaling to
    others, 18
potassium bromate, 149–50
Pottery Barn, 65
prAna, 63
previously incarcerated employees, 128
Pride Pages, 140
Primark, 216
Primeblue, 95
product returns, 89, 90
products, environmental impact of, 80
propylparaben, 149
Prosperity Candles, 66, 125
Publix, 130
Purl Soho, 63
PVH Corps, 70

Q

Quality Assurance International
(QAI), 174
quaternium-15, 161
quats, 164, 171
Queerly, 140

R

Rainforest Action Network, 86
Rainforest Alliance, 32, 35, 38, 49,
    76, 115
Rainforest Alliance Certified, 221
Rainforest Alliance (RA) Green Frog,
    64, 101
rainforest destruction, 80
Ralph Lauren, 67
RAN. *See* Rainforest Action Network
Rana Plaza factory building, collapse
    of, 48–49

ratings (systems, directories, and
    apps for), 69–72
RealReal, 211
recycling, 87
Red List (CSC), 158
Red No. 3, 148–49, 153
Red No. 40, 153
Re/Done, 214–15
Reformation, 216
Refugee Coffee Company, 142
refugee-owned businesses, 124, 125
Regeneration, 99
regenerative agriculture, 80, 102, 173
regenerative business practices, 94
regenerative materials, 215
regenerative movement, 99
Regenerative Organic Certified, 107
REI, 63, 211
reishi mushrooms, 94
Remake, 19, 49, 69, 70, 74, 111, 221
Renoon, 70
renting, 10, 204
Rent the Runway, 209
repair cafes, 210
repairs, 211
resale, 211
Responsible Jewelry, 68
Responsible Mica Initiative, 56, 68
Responsible Toys, 68
returns, 89, 90
Ridwell, 214
RMI. *See* Responsible Mica Initiative
Robin des Bois, 4
ROC. *See* Regenerative Organic
    Certified
R. Riveter, 125
rugs, 64–65

S

sale prices, 13
Sanchez, Susan, 127, 130
SBA. *See* U.S. Small Business
    Administration

scarcity, 14
SCJohnson, 188
SCS Global Services, 33
seafood
    certification of, 105
    mercury poisoning and, 153–56
    sustainable, 112
Seafood Task Force, 61
Seafood Watch (Monterey Bay
    Aquarium), 112
seed libraries, 210
Senreve, 94
Service Disabled Veteran Owned
    Small Business, 134
Seventh Generation, 93
SFI. *See* Sustainable Forestry Initiative
sharing economy, 207–11
sharing libraries, 210
Shopbipoc.com, 139
shopping habits, leading to lower
    expenses, 201–2
shopping high, 13–14
shopping with intention, 2–3
shopping models, new forms of, 10, 207
shopping superpower tips and tools, 38
    avoiding potential health hazards,
        169–84
    caring for the environment, 95–115
    community buying, 129–43
    principles of, 6–7
supporting employees, 58–75
shopping with your values, 12–13,
    14, 20–21
shrimp production, labor abuse in, 61
SIB-app, 208
Silent Spring Institute, 186
Simply Organic, 183
single-use plastics, 27, 96
Skin Carisma, 187
Skin Deep (EWG), 175, 185, 221
Skin Sort, 187

slavery, 49–52
Slow Food Snail of Approval, 105
Small Business Saturday, 137
Smart Label, 188
social washing, 25
sodium hydroxymethylglycinate, 161
sodium hypochlorite, 171
soil health, 85
Soko Farmers' Market app, 138, 139
Sopo Bikes, 211
South America, deforestation in, 85
spandex, 167
spider silk, 94
Sprouts, 130
Sri Lanka, mica mining in, 56
Starbucks, 33, 34, 38
Stella McCartney, 30
Stern Center for Sustainable Business
    (NYU), 197
storytelling, to avoid guilt, 17–20
subcontractors, 45
Substack, 141
sugarcane workers, abuse of, 41–42, 60
supply chains, 44–45, 62
    end-to-end, 183–84
    reporting and responding to
        abuse in, 54–56
    workers in, 47–49
Support Black Owned, 139
sustainable food, 106–7
Sustainable Forestry Initiative, 104
sustainable palm oil, 97
sustainable products, cost of, 10
swapping, 204

T
Tag Heuer, 33
take-back companies, 213–14
tanneries, 38, 53–54
Target, 35, 36, 63, 65, 101, 141, 173,
    203, 221
TEA. *See* triethanolamine
tea, switching buying habits for, 59
TerraCycle, 214

Terres des Hommes, 56
Thailand
    garment workers in, 74
    shrimp farming in, 61
    slaves in, 72
    tuna from, 61
The Gap, 67
The International Accord, 69
Theo Chocolate, 63
The Rug Company, 65
The Shoppers' Guide (EWG), 185
Think Dirty, 187
ThredUp, 211
Tide, 93
Timberland, 54
Timbuk2, 211
tires, reuse of, 94
Toad & Co., 183
Toblerone, 34
Tommy Hilfiger, 70
Tom's, 66, 106
Tony's Chocolonely, 54–55, 71
Too Good to Go, 111
tool libraries, 210
Tory Burch, 94
toxic chemicals, 147–48
toy libraries, 210
trade-offs, 24, 37–38, 198, 200–201
Trader Joe's, 44
transparency, 28, 54–55
Trashie.io, 213
travel apps, 138
triclocarbon, 162
triclosan, 162
triethanolamine, 161
Trip Advisor, 137, 138
tris(hydroxymethyl)nitromethane
    (Tris Nitro), 161
True Source Honey, 174
tuna, mercury exposure from, 154
U
UL GREENGUARD, 181
uncelebrated proprietors, 124–26
Uncommon Goods, 66

Unilever, 15, 92
United Nations Commission for
    Europe, 98
United Nations' Women's
    Empowerment Principles, 132
United States
    economy of, driven by consumer
        spending, 3
    Fair Packaging and Labeling Act,
        157
    slaves and child labor in, 49–50,
        52, 72
    water shortages in, 86
upcycling, 207, 214–15
up-front costs, factoring into
    purchases, 200–201
urbanization, 82
U.S. Black Chambers, Inc., 133
U.S. Cotton Trust Protocol, 67
U.S. Customs and Border Protection,
    51
USDA cage-free eggs, 173
USDA-certified grass-fed, 173
USDA-Certified Organic foods, 172–73
USDA-certified produce, 173
USDA Organic certification, 32, 49,
    100–103, 150–51, 159, 175, 221
U.S. Department of Energy, 100
U.S. Environmental Protection
    Agency, 89, 100, 154, 164
U.S. Food and Drug Administration,
    148
U.S. Small Business Administration,
    131, 134
Uyghurs, 51
V
vegan leather, 38
Veteran Disability Owned Business
Enterprises, 134
veteran-owned businesses, 124–25
Veteran Owned Businesses, 134

Veteran Owned Business Project, 138
Veteran Owned Small Businesses, 134
Victoria's Secret, 74
Virgin Group, 128
Virgin Hotels, 126–27
Vivienne Westwood, 99
VOB. *See* Veteran Owned Business
volatile organic compounds (VOCs),
    164–65, 181
Volkswagen, 29
Vosges Chocolate, 34
W
Walmart, 35–36, 99, 101, 173
Warby Parker, 66, 108
waste
    as Earth system, 81, 87–91
    high-impact switches for, 114
Waste Management, 214
water
    as Earth system, 81, 86–87
    efficient use of, shopping
        decisions and, 98
    high-impact switches for, 114–15
Watson, Emma, 30, 39
Watts, Naomi, 30
WBE. *See* Women's Business Enterprise
WBENC. *See* Women's Business
    Enterprise National Council
We Buy Black, 140, 221
WEConnect International, 139
Wegmans, 130
Weleda, 178
West Africa
    child labor in, 55, 59–60
    deforestation in, 85
West Elm, 65, 214
WFTO. *See* World Fair Trade
    Organization
WFTO Guarantee System, 67
Whole Foods Market, 99, 130
wildlife, risk to, 82

window cleaners, 189, 192
WOB. *See* Women-Owned Business
women, facing dangerous working
    conditions, 42
Women-Owned Business, 131
women-owned businesses, 9, 118–19,
    122, 123, 131
Women Owned Small Business, 131
Women's Business Enterprise, 131
Women's Business Enterprise
    National Council, 131, 139
wood products, 98, 104
workers
    abusive treatment of, 42–43
    brands' responsibility for, 43–44
    fair treatment of, indicators for, 57
    home-based, subject to
        exploitation, 45–46
    safety of, 48
    unfair treatment of, 47–48
World Fair Trade Organization,
    67–68
World Wide Fund for Nature, 86
World Wide Fund for Nature, Living
    Planet Report 2024, 82
WOSB. *See* Women Owned Small
    Business
WWF, 97
WWF. *See* World Wide Fund for
    Nature
X
Xinjiang province (China), 51–52
Y
Yelp, 137, 142
YouTube, 141
Yuka, 187
Yves Saint Laurent, 30

ACKNOWLEDGMENTS

Your Shopping Superpower is in your hands today because of work by many sustainability professionals during the last thirty years. Hard-headed visionaries have guided, nudged, and pushed companies to innovate, perform better, and be transparent. The sustainability tools relied upon today—supply chain management, climate strategy and carbon reduction goals, cross-sector partnerships, reporting, and many more—were developed by big thinkers and diligent doers, many of whom I'm honored to call colleagues and friends.

Thank you: Tom Cummings, Sheena Boughen, Paul Gilding and the Ecos clan, Paul Tebo, Janesse Brewer, Jason Clay, Cibele Salviatto, Jane Nelson, Andrea Spencer-Cooke, Fran van Dijk, David Grayson, Daniel Aronson, Doug Miller, Chris Coulter, NOW Partners, and colleagues in the early days at New Economics Foundation, Sustain-Ability, and BSR.

Immense gratitude for those who have helped advance safer labor conditions in supply chains and work to end slavery and child labor, including E. Benjamin Skinner, Fuzz and Carolyn Kitto, Matthew Friedman, Andrew Wallis, Julia Ormond, Alison Colwell, and many more who do the heavy lifting to end these crimes.

Thank you to Seth Godin and the Carbon Almanac Network. You are a source of great inspiration and encouragement to me.

Almost ten years ago, former president Bill Clinton and I were walking in Haiti, and he encouraged me to pursue my focus on consumers. Conversations with Gregory Milne, Donna Karan, Francine Lefrak, Joyce Lanigan, and many impact entrepreneurs fostered the spark of my idea.

Romy Fraser, Sandra Hill, and Daphne Lambert—your support and inspiration mean the world to me.

I heartfully thank members of the now extended Writing in Community, a group who shows up daily to virtually write together. Their gentle comments made this book better. A huge thanks to Shannon MacKinnon, Kerry Itami, Katy Dalgleish, Kathy Karn, Cynthia Miller, Annette Mason, Terri Tomoff, Cindy Villanueva, Regina Ochoa, Beverly Delidow, Julie B. Hughes, Kymberly Dakin-Neal, Melissa Balmer, Lori Sullivan, Heat Dziczek, Manon Doran, and the Cevennes Writers. A special shout-out goes to Louise Karch, for her unwavering support and whose book, *Word Glue,* led me to this book's title.

Beta-reading is unglamorous and laborious. My beta-readers are stars: Barbara-Anne Mansfield, Yvonne Daniel, Sabrina Kappler, and Constanza Montana. Claudine Beeson, Kerri Osmond, Gayle Gillig, and Alison Hastings read an early version and helped me reimagine the book. A massive thank you to Linda McLachlan for always saying yes to my requests for reviewing drafts and for her valuable insights. I can't thank Sally Burnheim enough for the detailed beta-reading and line editing of the entire manuscript multiple times. You're my hero!

Jenifer Anderson and Bridget Marnier helped keep all the pieces moving in the right direction. Thank you. Marnie and the Marniacs, what to say but a huge thank-you!

I am so thankful that Felice Della Gatta designed the infographics. You're brilliant, Felice! My agent, Laura Yorke, supported me throughout the process with grace. Thank you for believing in me and in this project. Darcie Abbene at HCI Books is a dream editor: collaborative and sharp. Thanks for making this a better book.

I could not have, and would not have, written this book without my in-house editor, sounding board, and love of my life, George Stenitzer. George, thanks for your endless support.

ABOUT THE AUTHOR

Diane discovered her shopping superpower while studying wild orangutans in Kalimantan, Indonesia. Watching the tropical forest cut down before her eyes, she understood in a flash that if no one bought products made from tropical wood, there would be no market for this timber and the deforestation would stop. This simple realization fueled her desire to earn a PhD in environmental economics at the London School of Economics and become an authority on sustainable and ethical products.

Sustainability isn't just her work. It's her passion.

For more than thirty years, she has helped companies create products that are better for the planet. She also collaborated to build many of the verification systems for sustainability certifications and reporting standards that millions of consumers rely upon today.

She's a nerd with a knack for translating complex issues into simple words. She is a coauthor with Seth Godin on the bestselling *The Carbon Almanac* (Penguin, 2022) and writes for many online journals and academic publications. Her consultancy, Osgood Consulting (https://dianeosgood.com), helps companies prepare for climate change and avoid human rights risks.

To connect with Diane, go to